Cambridge Elements

Elements in Theatre, Performance and the Political
edited by
Trish Reid
University of Reading
Liz Tomlin
University of Glasgow

PERFORMING URBAN ECOLOGIES

Lisa Woynarski
University of Reading

Shaftesbury Road, Cambridge CB2 8EA, United Kingdom

One Liberty Plaza, 20th Floor, New York, NY 10006, USA

477 Williamstown Road, Port Melbourne, VIC 3207, Australia

314–321, 3rd Floor, Plot 3, Splendor Forum, Jasola District Centre, New Delhi – 110025, India

103 Penang Road, #05–06/07, Visioncrest Commercial, Singapore 238467

Cambridge University Press is part of Cambridge University Press & Assessment, a department of the University of Cambridge.

We share the University's mission to contribute to society through the pursuit of education, learning and research at the highest international levels of excellence.

www.cambridge.org
Information on this title: www.cambridge.org/9781009565745

DOI: 10.1017/9781009443074

© Lisa Woynarski 2025

This publication is in copyright. Subject to statutory exception and to the provisions of relevant collective licensing agreements, no reproduction of any part may take place without the written permission of Cambridge University Press & Assessment.

When citing this work, please include a reference to the DOI 10.1017/9781009443074

First published 2025

A catalogue record for this publication is available from the British Library

ISBN 978-1-009-56574-5 Hardback
ISBN 978-1-009-44311-1 Paperback
ISSN 2753-1244 (online)
ISSN 2753-1236 (print)

Cambridge University Press & Assessment has no responsibility for the persistence or accuracy of URLs for external or third-party internet websites referred to in this publication and does not guarantee that any content on such websites is, or will remain, accurate or appropriate.

For EU product safety concerns, contact us at Calle de José Abascal, 56, 1°, 28003 Madrid, Spain, or email eugpsr@cambridge.org

Performing Urban Ecologies

Elements in Theatre, Performance and the Political

DOI: 10.1017/9781009443074
First published online: November 2025

Lisa Woynarski
University of Reading

Author for correspondence: Lisa Woynarski, l.woynarski@reading.ac.uk

Abstract: With the majority of the global population living in cities, urbanisation and climate crisis have become urgent planetary issues. This Element examines 'urban eco-performance', exploring how theatre and performance intersect with urbanisation and ecological crises to reimagine equitable urban futures. Through rigorous ecodramaturgical analyses, this Element critiques the colonial and capitalist systems shaping cities and highlights performance's role in addressing climate justice. Performances from Canada, Mexico, Nigeria, Taiwan, UK and USA, as well as Indigenous performances, are brought together for the first time to examine how they challenge the human/nature divide, revealing cities as vibrant ecological spaces. These performances foreground underrepresented voices and reframe cities as 'bio-urban' spaces. This Element integrates decolonial and intersectional ecological frameworks over three thematic sections: Living Cities, Petro-Cities and Urban Futures Against the Apocalypse. It argues for justice for marginalised communities while envisioning cities as interconnected ecosystems that can foster collective action and ecological resilience.

Keywords: performance and ecology, ecodramaturgy, environmental justice, cities and climate change, decolonising urban ecologies

© Lisa Woynarski 2025

ISBNs: 9781009565745 (HB), 9781009443111 (PB), 9781009443074 (OC)
ISSNs: 2753-1244 (online), 2753-1236 (print)

Contents

Introduction: Towards Urban Eco-Performance   1

1 Living Cities   12

2 Petro-cities   29

3 Urban Futures against the Apocalypse   47

Conclusion: Imagining a City   63

References   66

Introduction: Towards Urban Eco-Performance

Imagine driving on a highway overpass in your city. Through the guard rails, you glimpse a thriving working farm beneath you. To your surprise, there are school children, artists and local community members tending to gardens growing squash, lettuce, corn, potatoes and cabbage. Chickens, ducks, rabbits and sheep roam the site without cages. The San Francisco Mime Troupe is rehearsing their guerilla theatre there, while local young people are creating their own theatre for the stage on the site, and an Indigenous group is setting up for their powwow. Concrete, busy traffic and abandoned warehouses surround this six-point-five-acre farm under Highway 101. The juxtaposition of a thriving farm in a busy city landscape punctuates your typical image of urban living. This was *Crossroads Community: The Farm* (1974–1980) in San Francisco, created by performance artist Bonnie Ora Sherk. Today it is the site of Potrero del Sol Park, with a large skatepark, a performance space and community gardens, inspired by the legacy of *The Farm*.

We are now living on an urban planet, as more than half the world's population lives in cities (United Nations 2023). Cities are not merely geographical locations, rather they shape the lives of those who live in and around them – socially, politically and ecologically. They are both accelerators of climate change and subject to some of the greatest effects of the climate crisis. Structural inequalities, power imbalances and discrimination mean that already vulnerable and marginalised people are affected disproportionately by the asymmetrical social and ecological impacts. Compounding the threat of the climate crisis is the dominant ideological thinking that separates cities from 'nature', namely capitalism in different iterations (Smith 2008). Holding cities apart from the natural world is not only inaccurate in terms of the environmental impact created by urbanisation and resource use, but it also intensifies the effects of climate change. Cities are intimately interconnected to the more-than-human world (a term used to signal 'non-human' life, in a non-anthropocentric way).

The development of cities has changed the face of the earth. Urban theorist Herbert Girardet argues that rapid and increased urbanisation is 'fundamentally changing the condition of humanity and our relationship to the earth' (2008: 2). While agriculture and farming historically affected the landscape, urban development relies on fossil fuels and operates at an industrial scale, having unprecedented impacts on the planet. Humans have moved from farms and villages to large urban centres and megacities in a relatively short space of time. Previous focus on local resources has shifted to globally available resources, connecting cities to far-flung places. Urban growth has also meant an increase in slum living and informal settlements, particularly in the Global South. This has created horizontal networks of trade and commerce juxtaposed by vertical networks of social strata. This necessitates a focus on climate justice and equality in any thinking about urban ecologies and futures.

This Element analyses theatre and performance practices that are engaged in the urgent twin problems of urbanisation and climate crisis. Through an eco-dramaturgical analysis of a diverse range of performances, I ask what the role of theatre and performance is in reimagining urban ecologies. My argument unfolds over the course of three sections. First, I contend that urban eco-performances, at small scales, can recognise the aliveness (or material agency) of the city, being deeply embedded in nature as well as haunted by the ghosts of colonialism in cities of empire such as London. Then, I trace the global commodity of oil across three performances (from London to Nigeria and back to London) to understand the way colonialism and capitalism structure cities above all else, and the cultures that resist them. Finally, I turn to performances that imagine urban futures, opposing apocalyptic narratives, drawing on Indigenous knowledge and community-centred action. Foregrounding under-represented perspectives from cities around the globe, this Element addresses the question of how living in cities (for humans and more-than-humans) can be reimagined in more just and equitable ways in and through performance.

Whether divided by race or class or natural features such as rivers or mountains, cities reflect the inequalities of society at large. They also embody historic nature/culture divides, histories of displacement, discrimination and dispossession, anthropocentrism and material inequalities. This represents the uneven development which Neil Smith calls 'the hallmark of the geography of capitalism' (2008: 4). Cities represent vital landscapes for intersectional ecological thought, yet theatre and performance have been mostly absent from ecological urbanism studies. This work seeks to address this gap, analysing how performances of urban ecologies can help to imagine more ecologically just ways of living together.

This research began several years ago in response to a pervasive stereotype surrounding performance work that engages with ecology. Much of this work appeared to revolve around a narrow set of practices, which seem to exalt the countryside as 'authentic' nature or were designed to scare people through climate change lectures or post-apocalyptic narratives.[1] The countryside, within this context, was often framed as a morally 'pure' space that needed protection from urbanisation. While I acknowledge the necessity of rural land, this binary struck me as reductive. The countryside is far from pure. Agricultural practices

---

[1] Performance work engaged with ecology and climate has been expanding recently to include a diversity of different practices across multiple scales. See, for example, Beer 2021a; Ryan 2023; Spalink 2024.

frequently pollute soil and groundwater through the use of fertilisers and pesticides. Industrial-scale agriculture consumes vast quantities of water and contributes significantly to climate change—consider, for instance, the felling of forests to create farmland. Socially, rural spaces are often sites of exclusion and discrimination, as exemplified by the hostile experiences of Black communities in the USA and UK, as discussed in Section One. Living in the city, I found this anti-urban bias puzzling. My own experience complicated the nature/urban dichotomy: I lived beside one of Europe's largest city farms, and my commute home from the Underground often involved passing by horses, pigs, and sheep— in London Zone 2!

Performance in and of cities can enact ecological narratives, experiences and histories, replacing the clichéd image of eco-performance as a reverential walk through a 'green and pleasant land'. Theatre and performance offer novel experiences and new ways of viewing cityscapes, reflecting on (and potentially intervening in) the rife inequalities in global cities, which continue to be magnified by the climate crisis.

Bio-Urban

Performing Urban Ecologies theorises how new visions of the city are imagined, enacted and catalysed in performance. Urban coexistence invites us to rethink our relationships with urban spaces and inhabitants, both human and more-than-human. Urban growth and sprawl are indisputably ecologically destructive, often sacrificing green spaces for unsustainable commercial development, overconsuming resources and making cities less livable. Within this context, there is an opportunity to reconceptualise the city as an ecologically vibrant or what I term 'bio-urban' space (Woynarski 2020b). Inspired by thinkers such as David Harvey, who famously said there is nothing unnatural about New York City (1993: 28), this concept highlights the material aliveness of urban assemblages. Bio comes from the Greek root meaning living or life. By understanding the bio-urban relationships in a city, we can reshape our understanding of cities as part of 'nature', rather than stuck in a human/nature dualism, fostering more inclusive ecological urban development and contemporary city living.

The Western theatre has also played a role in reinforcing the urban/nature separation, often reducing nature to scenery for human action. For Una Chaudhuri (1995), this has created a 'negative theatre ecology' in modern Western drama, where the environment is often decontextualised, abstracted and aestheticised. Many canonical Western plays depict cities as spaces devoid of nature (i.e. *As You Like It, She Stoops to Conquer, Death of a Salesman*, etc.). As this kind of theatre is entrenched in a humanist tradition, it reinforces anthropocentrism in which 'nature' acts as a metaphor for human emotions. This theatre is considered an urban invention and metropolitan cultural signifier, further reflecting the reductive division. Theatre and cultural organisations can also have an ambivalent relationship to urban ecologies, through their locations in certain neighbourhoods, production processes and the way in which they produce the urban experience (on and off stage).

Despite the humanist tradition, I argue that performance practices can play a pivotal role in this reframing by revealing the vibrancy and agency of the more-than-human world. The anti-urban bias in ecological rhetoric reinforces harmful binaries between urban/nature and human/nature, justifying exploitative practices. This ultimately underpins the climate crisis because of the lack of understanding of how human life is connected to and reliant on other forms of life. The bio-urban concept resists these dualisms, proposing a living city where humans and more-than-humans actively participate in socio-ecological relationships. Viewing the city as part of a complex entanglement of living relationships that we share with humans and more-than-humans is essential to redefining growth and development, collapsing ideological distinctions, and promoting sustainable, inclusive urbanism. The bio-urban reaches towards an understanding of the myriad of unequal ecological relationships and climate impacts that make up a city, and the way they often affect the already vulnerable or marginalised. Through performance, we can further explore and challenge these relationships, illuminating not only the global ecological impacts of large-scale urbanisation, but the ecological vibrancy inherent to urban living.

Intersectional ecologies

In the following, I theorise the way performance engages with interconnected social, political and ecological issues, highlighting the entangled nature of these issues in contemporary cities. The performances included in this Element range in geographies from the UK to Nigeria, the USA, Taiwan, Canada and Mexico. I understand these performance works as intersectional in that they invest in and foreground marginalised people, voices and more-than-human actants in their contexts. What I call intersectional ecologies (Woynarski 2020a, 2020b) acknowledge the way in which the slow violence of ecological destruction is intimately interconnected with other forms of violence (Nixon 2013). I argue that an intersectional ecological perspective is a necessary addition to any ecological thinking, particularly given the complexity, scale and histories of cities.[2]

---

[2] Intersectional analysis calls for an acknowledgement of my own position. I situate my knowledge as a Canadian-born, UK-based, urban-dwelling white woman who is a theatre and performance scholar and educator. These aspects of my identity influence my perspective.

My conception of intersectional ecologies (Woynarski 2020b) within urban living draws on Rebecca Solnit's (2006) articulation of the connection between Jane Jacobs's city planning, Rachel Carson's environmentalism and Betty Friedan's feminism, all contemporaries published in the early 1960s.[3] Jacobs influential and now classic book, *The Death and Life of Great American Cities* (1992 [1961]), problematised the then dominant planning paradigms of 'modern' cities, designed on principles of separation, segregation and auto-centrism, which deepened inequalities rather than addressed them. Instead, Jacobs posited a city supported by diversity principles of (working-class) communities and mixed-use spaces. Similarly, Friedan's *The Feminine Mystique* (1963) was a response to the conditions created by the separation and isolation Jacobs wrote about (American women's gendered suburban disaffection). Solnit connects these two projects to Carson's *Silent Spring* (2000 [1962]), which is credited with popularising modern American environmentalism. 'Together, these three writers addressed major facets of the great modern project to control the world on every scale, locating it in the widespread attacks on nature, on women and on the chaotic, the diverse, the crowded and the poor' (Solnit 2006). Revisioning the city in ways that work for all people means acknowledging the ecology and the effects of urbanisation, while, at the same time, working towards equality and access for all, questioning the dominant logic of neoliberal capitalism, colonialism and the modern project of 'control'. These ideas are exemplified in the performances included in this Element.

All three of the above authors were white American women, whose work is not without problematic elements or missing perspectives: Friedan's omission of the experiences of women of colour and working-class women who may have been in the workforce out of necessity and Jacob's idealisation of white working-class neighbourhoods without sufficient acknowledgement of the role social and financial capital play in structural inequalities. Despite these shortcomings and the complicated legacies of their work, each writer addressed marginalisation in some form. By bringing these three projects together, Solnit is gesturing towards intersectional ecologies where ecological destruction disproportionately affects women, the poor, people of colour, Indigenous peoples, disabled people and other marginalised people and is therefore tied to other forms of violence, political power and social mobility. Read together, these three thinkers suggested a need for reimagining city life as diverse and ecologically vibrant, in ways which work for all communities (including the more-than-human) based on principles of access, equality and liberation. Bringing a contemporary intersectional perspective to their work forms a central idea of the performing urban ecologies:

---

[3] This material was first published in Woynarski 2020b.

ecological issues are innately connected to social and political structures that shape urban life in uneven and unjust ways.

Conceptualising the City

In the vast body of work that makes up urban studies and the study of cities, I am particularly concerned with the relationship between the urban, the ecological and the asymmetrical impacts of climate change. The city I am referring to is not a fixed locale or concept. As geographers Amin and Thrift (2002) assert, 'cities have become extraordinarily intricate, and for this, difficult to generalise. We can no longer even agree on what counts as a city' (1). This sentiment echoes through urban theory, where definitions of cities and the urban are disputed. Shifting and ambiguous geographies, demographics and ways of categorising cities mean there are competing and debatable ideas of what constitutes a city. For Amin and Thrift, 'the city is everywhere and in everything' (2002: 1). Brenner points to Louis Wirth's famous (although slightly outdated) definition of city from the 1930's, based on three features: 'large population size, high population density, and high levels of demographic heterogeneity' (Brenner 2013: 90). Although these features may be found in numerous cities across the globe, the triad misses out on the complexity of theorising the multiplicity of cities today.

Among the different concepts of cities and the urban, there are a few that resonate with this project of theorising performances of urban ecologies. Heynen et al. (2006) suggest, 'cities are dense networks of interwoven sociospatial processes that are simultaneously local and global, human and physical, cultural and organic' (1), making them both part of nature and constructed through human means. Doreen Massey writes that cities have specific spatial features – 'a region of particularly dense networks of interaction' – and it is their density and juxtaposition of difference that characterises them (1999: 156). According to Smith, the geography of the urban is 'determined by the local labor market and the limits to the daily commute' (2008: 183). For Amin and Lancion, 'cities are entanglements of bodies, nature, things, technologies, infrastructures, and institutions' (2022: 1). Nicholas Whybrow argues that the city functions as an 'ecological' body referring to a metaphorical sense of 'the circulation of particular socio-economic and cultural discourses' (2011: 8). I extend Whybrow's concept of the city as an ecological body by focusing on the literal ecological relationships (which include the socio-economic and cultural) of urban living.

For my purposes, I understand the urban as the spatial, social and ecological processes that extend far beyond their immediate geographical location and are structured and propped up by systems of exploitation and extraction (namely capitalism and colonialism). While carefully demarcating the borders or parameters of urban or city sites is not my concern, the material conditions and processes that produce urban living conditions are. The city is made up of entanglements (Amin and Lacione 2022) of power and 'dense networks of interaction' (Massey 1999: 156) for both humans and more-than-humans. These interactions are social, political and ecological. Understanding how these are connected and the far-reaching effects of some of these interactions is where I argue performance can intervene.

I draw on urban political ecology to examine the ways in which socio-ecological conditions are produced and experienced in the city. For theorists Ernstson and Swyngedouw, urban political ecology 'focuses on the uneven urbanization of nature, the socio-ecological inequalities that pattern cities, and the perplexing socionatural landscapes that capitalist urbanization produces within, between and beyond cities' (Ernstson and Swyngedouw 2019: 4). Urban political ecology theory is a useful extension to intersectional ecologies, bringing the specificity of urban contexts to my ecodramaturgical performance analysis. Particular insights include how social mobility or agency determines in which neighbourhoods waste treatment centres were built in New York City, highlighted by Mierle Laderman Ukeles performance work with the New York Sanitation Department in Section One.

Thinking towards sustainable and liveable cities, Girardet offers a definition of a sustainable city as one that 'enables all its citizens to meet their own needs and to enhance their well-being, without degrading the natural world or the lives of other people, now or in the future' (2008: 6). Inequalities, which led to asymmetrical impacts of climate change, are at the centre of what needs to be addressed to make liveable cities. Intersectional ecological thinking asks questions about who has access to public spaces, housing and culture. This includes safe and affordable housing as well as equal access to opportunities and freedom from discrimination. Girardet highlights how liveability needs to foreground access to culture, particularly in cities with high-profile cultural industries such as London, New York and Paris, where 'many people can't afford to go to concerts, the theatre or the opera. A liveable city makes sure that these issues are addressed and that the participation of all people in a diverse variety of cultural activities is assured ... trees, plants and animals also need their distinct urban habitats' (Girardet 2008: 15). Access and participation in the city are important for addressing inequalities and marginalisation.

It is not possible to generalise all cities – there are so many varying types of scales, landscapes, geo-political structures, populations, etc. The complexity of cities and their relationship to the more-than-human world are relatively specific to their geographies. My aim is to pull out some of the specific circumstances of the performances and the cities in which they are located to highlight commonalities and theorise the ways in which performance can help us think through uneven urban ecologies.

Indigenous Urbanism

A central concern of this Element is making visible how colonialism has structured cities and continues to shape patterns of exclusion and marginalisation. The future of liveable or sustainable cities needs to be premised on decolonisation. Like the prevalent urban/nature binary, there is another false dualism that juxtaposes the city and Indigeneity[4]. Perhaps this is because of the pervasive stereotype of Indigenous peoples' association with 'traditional' ways of living, often on 'the land' or on reservations or rural or remote settings. Anishinaabe geographer Heather Dorries writes that an Indigenous urban theory is needed because 'in Canada, the terms Indigeneity and urbanity have been configured by colonialism and are often understood as antithetical' (2023: 110). This is the case for other settler-colonial nations as well. Dorries draws on Glen Coulthard's (Yellowknives Dene) term 'urbs nullius' (2014: 176) as a way of signalling how cities and urban landscapes are imagined as spaces without Indigenous peoples. 'Much like the concept "terra nullius", which imagined the lands of the new world devoid of human inhabitants and available for settlement, according to the logic of "urbs nullius", the presumed disappearance and assimilation of Indigenous peoples paves the way for urbanisation' (Dorries 2023: 111–112). Urbanisation then facilitates the end goal of the settler colonial project of Indigenous erasure and dispossession.

Dorries argues for an Indigenous urbanism that foregrounds the opposing ideas of Indigeneity and urbanism and understands them as 'constantly in flux and open to contestation' (2023: 110). Dorries contends that the urban can be both liberatory and discriminatory for Indigenous peoples and that performance can play a role in its liberatory potential. She writes that 'Indigenous peoples are also using artistic practices to articulate urban Indigenous identity' (2023: 144) through decolonial aesthetics, asserting Indigenous presence in the city. For example, artist collective Ogimaa Mikana, founded by Anishinaabe artists Susan Blight and Hayden King, makes site-specific interventions into urban landscapes to reclaim Indigenous urban existence. Started during an Idle No More protest in 2013, their work has involved returning street names in Toronto

---

[4] 'Indigenous' is used to indicate a shared history of colonial violence, rather than a homogenising identity. Nations, cultures and tribes are specified, where available, usually in brackets after the name of an author.

(or *Tkaronto* in the Mohawk language) to their Anishinaabe language. What began as a clandestine intervention of replacing some street signs was adopted officially by the City of Toronto in 2016. Spadina Road was returned to the name 'Ishpadinaa', meaning 'place on a hill'. Later, the City officially installed a street sign with 'Ishpadinaa' listed above the English-language name. Three other major roads also had the Anishinaabe language addition, asserting the ongoing Indigenous presence in the heart of the city. Ogimaa Mikana's work has also extended to billboards, historical plaques, street art and banners on buildings. Blight describes the ethos of their urban site interventions as asserting 'Anishinaabe self-determination on the land and in the public sphere' (Blight 2018). Their work embodies the fissures that performance interventions can make in the settler colonial logic of cities.

The analysis of the city through colonialism (past and ongoing) is an animating principle of this Element. In Section One, I analyse Peter Morin's *Cultural Graffiti in London* as a street performance that makes visible the colonial systems and monuments that shape the city. The effects of settler colonialism on oil extraction in Canada and Nigeria (financed through London) is the subject of Section Two. In Section Three, I examine Yvette Nolan's (Algonquin) play *The Unplugging* and the type of future the play imagines based on Indigenous principles and ways of knowing. These works emphasise how colonialism patterns cities and gesture to a future of cities based on decolonisation, equality and access.

Urban Eco-Performance

This Element focuses on urban performance encounters across multiple scales. These range from momentary or temporary encounters to larger-scale performances. I use the term performance (and sometimes theatre) to refer to an event/experience/encounter. This can include watching a play on stage, but most examples refer to site-based or spatialised performances. I find resonance with eco-theatre scholar Courtney Ryan's spatialised eco-performance in which she writes 'contextualized and multiscalar micro-performances can, in small but meaningful ways, expose much larger forces of extractive capitalism and micromanagement, revealing the ways in which every environmental act has multiple, unseen ecological consequences' (Ryan 2023: 9). Her concept allows for a focus on the spatial dimensions of performance which in turn draws a focus on spatialised justice. I also endeavour to mobilise urban eco-performance to reveal the 'multiple, unseen ecological consequences' of planetary urbanisation. Although there are several site-based performance examples included below, this is not to imply that site-based work is inherently ecological or engaging in urban ecologies. Site-based performance practices do, however, often allow for a specificity of place, in terms of audience experience, that can be harder to achieve on stage. The performances detailed in this Element are encounters that allow an audience to experience urban ecological landscapes or relationships in new ways. Whether this is creating a working farm under a highway overpass, restoring a forgotten creek in a commuter city or voting on future ways of living in cities together, the audience who encounter these works may gain a new perspective on the uneven and precarious urban relationships that make up their city.

The constellation of performances featured here has been chosen because they represent urban encounters set apart from the everyday. Taken together, they provide a succinct (although limited) encapsulation of urban eco-performances spanning the 1970s until 2023. In the short format of this Element, it would be impossible to provide an extensive and detailed overview. Therefore, I have sampled from the archive and chosen works that are novel in form or dramaturgical features or location or narrative, or that speak to different facets of urban ecologies. I am specifically interested in how these performances illuminate the invisible capitalism and colonial structures of the cities in which they take place.

I use an ecodramaturgical analysis to unravel how the performances included here draw out the connections between urban living and the climate crisis. As articulated in my previous work, 'ecodramaturgies are a way of understanding how theatre and performance practices make ecological meaning and interact with the material more-than-human world, attendant to the different experiences, complexities and injustices that entails' (Woynarski 2020a: 10). This work considered a variety of contemporary ecologically orientated performances with the aim of expanding the field of performance and ecology and the relationship between theatre and climate change. Here, my focus shifts to a shorter form to develop a specific area within the field of performance and ecology: performances of urban ecologies and climate justice, to understand how performance speaks to this planetary condition.

Drawing on Theresa J May's concept of ecodramaturgy[5] I extend my analysis to a variety of performance practices, thinking specifically about urban ecological contexts. For May 'ecodramaturgy examines the role of theatre in the face of rising ecological crises, foregrounding the material ecologies represented on stage' (May 2020: 4). Her work gives a deep focus to the American theatre and the complex and fluid socio-environmental conditions in US contexts. While I look to different geographies and cities (the United States but also the United Kingdom, Canada, Nigeria, Mexico and Taiwan) and work outside

---

[5] Also, Arons and May 2012; Eckersall et al. 2014; Thomas 2016; Lavery 2018; Angelaki 2019; Blissett 2021; Ahmadi 2022; Ryan 2023; Spalink 2024.

'the stage', I continue to take inspiration from May's foregrounding and platforming of Indigenous stories, voices and perspectives. Including Indigenous perspectives and highlighting the connection between colonialism and the climate crisis is a key aim of this Element.

Each section below focuses on a dynamic set of performance examples to interpret distinct aspects of urban ecologies, adopting different spatio-temporal points of view and varied but connected methodologies. *Section One: Living Cities* examines four performances spread across four global cities: Bonnie Ora Sherk's *The Farm* (San Francisco 1974–1980), Mierle Laderman Ukeles' work at the New York Sanitation Department (1976-present), Wu Mali's *Plum Tree Creek* project (New Taipei City 2011–2013) and Peter Morin's (Tahltan Nation) *Cultural Graffiti in London* (2013). This spread of work highlights different aspects of the living relationships that make up a city, including farms, sanitation labour and waste, lost community waterways and the ongoing effects of colonialism. *Section Two: Petro-cities* takes a linear journey tracing the global commodity of oil and its transformations along the way, from where it is financed in London to where it is extracted in the Niger Delta and then to a Nigerian-diaspora climate activist in London. Three performances trace the constellation of relationships that underpin petro-cities and how the global oil trade affects them: *Oil City* (Evans and Platform 2013), Eke's *Shields* (2006), and *Can I Live?* (Balogun 2021). In *Section Three: Urban Futures Against the Apocalypse*, the focus shifts to imagining spaces of urban futures against the typical apocalyptic narratives that have dominated cultural representations. Instead of doomsday representations, I consider what futures could look like based on Indigenous principles in Yvette Nolan's *The Unplugging* (2014), through community participation and intervention in Fast Familiar's *The Strategy Room* (2023, UK) and in access to urban green spaces in Mexico City in Aris Pretelin-Esteves' *Proyecto TEJIDOS (*2018–2022). This section reimagines geographical connections (and journeys), re-mapping space for possible futures through community action.

Planetary urbanisation has seen an unprecedented transformation of the more-than-human world. With that have come the unequal effects of environmental devastation on the most vulnerable. This includes an increase in floods, forest fires, mudslides, hurricanes, heat waves and drought, bringing with them famine, war and displacement. Brenner starkly relates the scale and impact of mass planetary urbanisation, which 'is now recognized as contributing directly to far-reaching transformations of the atmosphere, biotic habitats, land-use surfaces, and oceanic conditions that have long-term implications for the metabolism of both human and nonhuman life-forms' (2013: 86). Climate change and urban growth have had unprecedented effects on the earth. My hope is that the silos that have historically separated urban studies, environmentalism and the arts will start to crack open as we tackle this transformation and imagine alternative ways of living in cities together.

1 Living Cities

Cities are teeming with life. We might think of the crowds of people en route to work, the dull hum of seemingly endless construction, the vibrations of underground trains below the street, or the crush of traffic-filled roads jammed with lorries, buses and taxi cabs, people walking dogs or surprisingly quiet cemeteries. We might not think of the complex ecosystems of more-than-human species, systems and processes that also make up urban living. Cows, pigs and chickens mingle with artists and children as they tend crops on a farm under a highway overpass; observers track garbage trucks and follow their contents to the landfill; community members share a seasonal, locally grown breakfast together in a dense urban area; an Indigenous man sings to colonial monuments as palace guards look on. Though these images may not be typically associated with the city, they are performance acts that reveal the complex ecological vibrancy within urban areas.

As indicated in the Introduction, the city is both 'natural' and human-influenced and created. Urban geographers Lisa Benton-Short and John Rennie Short describe the city as a hybrid space that is 'both an environmental and a social construct. The city is an integral part of nature and nature is intimately interwoven into the social life of cities ... The city is a site where the emergent connections between the political and the ecological are revealed and contested' (2013: 2). The hybrid space of the city creates some friction that then reveals the complex intersectional ecological relationships that govern more than half of the global population's urban living conditions (albeit in very different ways depending on the specific city). The performance interventions in this section demonstrate how these relationships can be re-imagined, even at a micro-scale or for a limited time, to foster more just urban ecologies.

This section examines the way performance can demonstrate and interrogate the city as part of 'nature', home to vital, living ecosystems. The four performance works included here highlight the tensions of experiencing the city as a living environment which supports (or fails to support) a large, diverse human and more-than-human population. They also model how cities can be planned and inhabited in ways that acknowledge and foster material aliveness, or what I refer to as bio-urban. I have chosen these works from the archive because of how pioneering they are as urban eco-performance. I analyse Bonnie Ora Sherk's *The Farm* (San Francisco 1974–1980) and Mierle Laderman Ukeles' work at the New York Sanitation Department (1976-present) as intersectional urban eco-performance, extending previous studies of their work as feminist environmental performance art.[6] These works, together with Wu Mali's *Plum Tree Creek* project (Taiwan 2011–2013), revise and redefine human/more-than-human relationships and interactions, conceiving of an urban community as made up of multiple species and people. These influential women artists provide models for radical coexistence, breaking down reductive urban/nature and nature/culture binaries. Indigenous performances that tap into long (and often hidden) histories of cities of empire foreground how legacies of colonialism are living in the structures of contemporary cities, as with Peter Morin's (Tahltan Nation) *Cultural Graffiti in London* (2013). Taken together, these works offer multiple ways of viewing the city as alive, providing new insights into the concept of the bio-urban. Recontextualising these performance works through an intersectional ecological analysis, I argue they act as key sites for addressing critical issues of race, class, gender, colonisation and environmental justice in their cities.

The Farm

As described in the Introduction, the location of Sherk's farm, called Crossroads Community, was a derelict six-and-a-half-acre cement site surrounded by a busy freeway interchange on San Francisco's then Army Street and empty warehouses. Funded by public money available for the creation of open spaces after the completed development of the motorway interchange, *The Farm* was a working farm that was also part social experiment and part community art project. It operated between 1974 and 1980. Sherk eventually built up the site to include a garden, farm, park, school without walls, alternative art space, performance space, community centre, environmental education centre, cafe, kitchen, library and more. Visitors, artists (including the San Francisco Mime Troupe), community members and local school groups ran and maintained the farm, learning to grow food and tend to the more than seventy animals that lived there.

The Farm's structure and location countered the reductive dualism that separates humans from their environment or 'nature', and puts the urban (human's place) in opposition to nature. Sherk articulates the bio-urban concept in *The Farm*'s ethos: 'everything found in the country is implicit in the city. Urban environments today, however, due in part to technological excesses, fragment our spaces and lives so that we have difficulty experiencing whole

---

[6] I have previously written about Sherk's *The Farm* and Ukeles' New York Sanitation Department work in Woynarski 2020b, where some of this material first appeared.

systems' (Sherk 2012: 165). *The Farm* was a bio-urban performance work that recognised the aliveness of the living world within the built environment, which can illuminate or activate radical ways of human and more-than-human coexistence. Tending to crops while living in dense urban housing, surrounded by motorways, was made compatible for the community members involved, although a small-scale temporary intervention.

The city and the country divide has racial undertones, particularly in the USA and the UK. Cultural geographer Carolyn Finney argues that the national sentiment of 'the countryside implicitly excluded black people' (2014: 7). This is opposed to the city, in which the euphemism 'urban' often operates as an euphemism for Black people and culture (Brown 2020). Finney argues that the 'country' and related 'nature' activities, such as hiking, birdwatching and camping, are coded as 'white' activities that exclude people of colour, perpetuated by a lack of representation. Whiteness becomes the dominant lens for environmentalism (Finney 2014: 3). In Britain, these harmful stereotypes are deeply ingrained, as musician VV Brown describes her experience as the sole Black woman living in a countryside village: 'The countryside is a territorial place, full of imperial nostalgia, that harks back to a time when black people were not welcome. The very concept of Britishness is wrapped up in images of the fields of England – and I do not represent that concept' (2020: n.p.). These reductive racial stereotypes are a further product of the problematic binary that separates the city from the more-than-human world. *The Farm* attempted to redress this harmful divide and attendant cultural stereotypes by making it a place for diverse local communities.

The area of *The Farm* was bordered by four neighbourhoods described by Sherk as 'low-income, high need' (Sherk cited in Galpin 2013: n.p.): Mission, Bernal Heights, Potrero Hill and Bayview communities. These San Francisco neighbourhoods were home to people of colour, immigrants, LGBTQIA+ people and counterculture movements such as artists and punks. The development of the highway in this area follows an infrastructure trend in the USA of building large-scale development projects through low-income neighbourhoods that further marginalise and separate the inhabitants. For L'Heureux, highways 'also bring pollution, lower air quality, create inequities, and ultimately perpetuate the legacies of racism' (2012: 103). Sherk envisioned *The Farm* as an experimental community and agricultural centre that could provide a small but significant corrective to the effects of the highway. 'In addition to wanting to develop a place where people could experience live animals, I saw this land configuration as a way to bring people from these diverse communities together, as well as plants and animals' (Sherk in Galpin 2013: n.p.). Diversity sat at the heart of *The Farm*, within it 'many people of different ages, backgrounds, and colours come and go, participating in and creating a variety of programmes which richly mix with the life processes of plants and animals' (Sherk 2012: 166). Sherk's concept of an urban agricultural space included a sense of intersectionality with the social, political, cultural and ecological elements of the area.

The Farm also provides an example of one of the core positions of the bio-urban: problematising a reductive idea that cities are not part of 'nature' or that they are less 'ecological' than the suburbs or rural areas. While the development of cities and urbanisation has a major environmental impact and requires outlying land to support them, cities can also be efficient at distributing resources due to their density. Cities can be home to great biodiversity and ecologically thriving spaces, as *The Farm* demonstrates. However, cities also produce pollutants and lots of waste, have poorer air quality and are major contributors to the climate crisis (Benton-Short and Rennie Short 2013: 7–8). Despite this, cities are not inherently less ecological than the countryside, particularly considering intensive, industrial agricultural practices in rural areas that can be ecologically damaging. *The Farm*'s biodiversity and efficient agricultural practices demonstrate the concept of the bio-urban by breaking down binaries in an acknowledgement that cities are a vibrant part of nature and the ecology of the more-than-human world. Cities are both 'nature' and 'culture'. *The Farm* hosted local children who would come to interact with animals, tend crops or take a dance class. Sherk offered gardening, agriculture, animals and an educational centre to the local communities while also attracting animals, insects and wildlife to the site. It is one example of how animals can be configured as part of urban ecologies. Sherk viewed the project as a way to explore the potential of alternative ways of coexisting in the city, through the integration of the surrounding neighbours, both human and more-than-human (2012: 166).

The Farm enacted an ecomaterialist perspective through its expansion of community and agency of food. Sherk's work considers a human urban dweller, not in opposition to the natural world, but always co-mingling with a multiplicity of species. Her vision was based on the idea that the site was alive with different materials and creatures. This ecomaterialist view acknowledges the agency of humans in an interdependent relationship with all the other vibrant matter of the site. Ecomaterialism aims to challenge binary thinking that supports the perception of the more-than-human world as something inanimate, devoid of agency or meaning and separate from human life, as in much Indigenous thought. I extend this thinking to the bio-urban to consider the way in which performance can manifest the vibrancy of the material world and ecological agency of the city, moving away from binaries towards intersectional ecological thinking. *The Farm* did this by conceptualising the city as alive, full of living processes and relationships, including urban food growing. Ecomaterialist philosopher Jane Bennett (2010: 42) refers to food as an 'operator', as it is an assemblage of 'things' and relationships: it creates effects through economics, transportation, pesticides, agribusiness and labour, soil, pollination, ingredients and sustenance, health and much more. *The Farm* also embodies urban ecological contradictions, as the scale of the farm was not enough to address systemic issues around food accessibility or pervasive urbanisation.

As the urban experience is quickly becoming one of the most prevalent, we must start thinking of the city as ecologically vibrant in order to reframe growth and development in ecological terms. Considering the way in which the city has ecological agency may help to understand urban development in social, political and ecological contexts. *The Farm* existed outside of the dominant capitalist system (formally as a non-profit public trust), providing a home for artists as well as food and education for the local communities. This was a form of cultural resistance, providing ways of conceiving of city life as resistant to the grand narrative of capitalist accumulation, reimagining what urban life could be for humans and more-than-humans. In 1981, *The Farm* was served with an eviction notice and the site was turned into a conventional park (La Raza Park and then Potrero del Sol Park), although it contains community gardens and artists' studios as a legacy of the project. The dominant planning paradigm reasserted itself, but for a brief time, *The Farm* was a bio-urban experiment that revealed the ecological vibrancy of the city, based on justice, equality and decommodification.

Mierle Laderman Ukeles' work at the New York Sanitation Department

Mierle Laderman Ukeles' feminist, intersectional ecological art practice focuses on the materiality of waste in New York City by making unseen waste management systems visible. She is (the first and only) artist in residence at the New York City Sanitation Department. Her work there has included *Touch Sanitation* (1979–80), in which she proceeded to shake hands with all 8,500 sanitation workers in the department, saying, 'Thank you for keeping New York City alive.' This action connects the vibrancy or aliveness of the city to the networks of often undervalued people and labour, waste materials and processing, making visible everyday ecological relationships.

Like Sherk, Ukeles' work re-envisions human/more-than-human relationships and interactions, conceiving of an urban 'community' as made up of multiple materials. Ukeles takes the usually unseen labour of maintenance work and recontextualises it within urban ecological terms. Her piece *Flow City* (1983–2001) involved plans for a visitor centre in the newly built 59th

Street Marine Transfer Station in Manhattan, where waste was unloaded from garbage trucks to barges and transferred to Fresh Kills Landfill on Staten Island via the Hudson River. Ukeles (1996, 2012) envisioned the centre as a 'public environment' with the aim of embedding art and public participation in the waste management system. Visitors would enter through a Passage Ramp made of recycled materials, including glass and rubber, and then proceed to a Glass Bridge. While the Glass Bridge was built as part of the transfer station that opened in 1996, the rest of *Flow City* remained imagined due to a lack of funding. Ukeles' detailed plans form much of the work. The bridge contained three very different views of the city: to the east was a panoramic view of the city skyline or the 'formal city with the icons of New York'; to the west were the trucks dumping their waste on the barges, passing under the bridge in the 'Violent Theatre of Dumping'; and to the south at the end of the bridge she planned a Media Flow Wall (Ukeles 2012: 42–43). Eco-arts scholar Don Krug wrote about this piece on the now-defunct Green Museum website. He described the three perspectives of the Glass Bridge, which 'provided a range of views for visitors to see and question everyday consumer choices and to learn more about the consequences of their lifestyle on creating a healthy environment in the future' (Krug 2006). These perspectives drew the attention of residents to the scale of the waste they produce and the labour it takes to process it, making visible what it takes to 'keep the city alive'.

The Media Flow Wall was envisioned to have twenty-four monitors encased in a crushed glass wall with video displays from scientists, ecologists, artists and local experts providing context on urban ecological issues and waste management. It would also include live footage from six cameras of the Hudson River outside and under the station (including underwater). As the site restricted access to the river, Ukeles wanted the presence of the river in the centre, as 'this river makes the city live' (Ukeles 2012: 43). The wall would also contain documentation of the garbage accumulating at Fresh Kills Landfill. She envisioned the wall as allowing visitors 'to pass "through" this physical point in order to get a broader understanding of how this kind of place links up with the systems of the planet' (Ukeles 2012: 43). Visual links between ecological relationships were to be created by juxtaposing the unseen work of garbage collection with images of its final destination in the landfill.

Ukeles' work demonstrates an important aspect of the bio-urban. In order to dissolve the dichotomy between the urban and 'nature', we must acknowledge that the ecological is not always (and perhaps not usually) verdant green spaces. Waste and garbage are as much a part of urban ecology as city parks and farms. The whole of a city is part of the more-than-human world and embedded in ecological relationships (that also have ethical, social, political and community dimensions). The social and political dimensions of ecology can be hidden or invisible when our image of 'nature' is limited to rolling green hills or anything 'green'. Urban areas are where many of these social–political–ecological relationships play out in our everyday lives. As landscape architect Michael Hough (2004) suggests, an underground public transportation system is an ecological system, and when we start to think of it as such, we may start to recognise its vibrancy and design. Ukeles' work contextualising the waste management system as an ecological system, facilitated by residents, sanitation workers, as well as more-than-human actants, helps us understand it as an ecological system that we are a part of, including the destructive consequences of our behaviour. Ukeles' work asks us to imagine what maintenance and care might be like if we valued it (outside of capitalist terms) and understood it as part of living ecologies in which we are always already participating.

Waste transfer stations are contentious topics in New York City since diesel trucks pollute the air, cause high rates of asthma, and the workers at the sites are often undertaking dangerous work for a low wage without unionisation, as environmental justice scholar Julie Sze has written (2007: 110–111). In 2001, NYC closed Fresh Kills Landfill (the largest landfill in the world), which was the last municipally operated landfill in the city. Privatisation of residential waste management meant more use of waste transfer stations located within the city. Garbage and waste management 'is an urban and racial matter, with political, economic, and geographical implications ... The neighbourhoods particularly vulnerable to changing garbage policies are poor and working-class neighbourhoods' (Sze 2007: 113). There is a higher proportion of putrescible waste transfer sites in low-income neighbourhoods, with more than half of them located in the South Bronx and Williamsburg/Greenpoint, with these sites handling 73 per cent of the cities' waste (114). Environmental justice activists in these neighbourhoods (with high populations of people of colour) have organised to ask 'important questions about the distribution of benefits and burdens of city services and how the allocation of these burdens and benefits was influenced by race, class, and politics' (116). Garbage is a lightning rod for many intersectional ecological issues in cities. David Harvey (1989) configures garbage as both a metaphor for disposable and fictitious capital, and material in the unevenly distributed waste management system. Garbage represents the global flow of capital and alienation with an emphasis on instantaneity and disposability. Workers are alienated from the products of their labour, many (affluent) residents are alienated from the consequences of their lifestyles and users of these objects are alienated from their disposal. 'In 2000, New York City residents and businesses generated approximately 43,000 to 45,000 tons of waste per day' (Sze 2007: 112). Ukeles' work aimed to connect people to invisible urban ecological relationships, recognising the way rubbish can never be thrown 'away', as it continues to exercise agency. Focused on the material effectiveness of waste and the issue of maintenance work, Ukeles' performance art highlights the inseparability and intersectionality of waste, ecology, labour and social structures in an urban context.

The pervasiveness of the nature/culture (and therefore human/nature and urban/nature) dichotomy has proven difficult to overcome, within scholarship and in how we interact and think about our relationship to the more-than-human world more generally. This is in part because both nature and culture have been deeply contested terms across history. The work of Sherk and Ukeles demonstrates how performance can dissolve this reductive dualism by shifting how we see human and more-than-human relationships, looking towards the bio-urban to convey a sense of the life and vibrancy of the ecological world. Although the sites of these works are in global American cities, the participation of underrepresented humans and more-than-humans opens them up to intersectional ecological readings. They are small-scale, radical examples that reveal the multiple socio-ecological relationships that make up a city.

Plum Tree Creek Project

2011: New Taipei City, Taiwan. Artist and curator Wu Mali[7] collaborated with Bamboo Curtain Studio to create a series of cultural actions at Plum Tree Creek in the Zhuwei neighbourhood. Her aim was to draw attention to the forgotten and neglected Plum Tree Creek that runs through the neighbourhood. Named for the plum trees that once grew on its banks, the creek was contaminated and no longer played a central role in urban life. Wu lived near the creek and was amazed to learn about the community it once served. She devised a programme of arts interventions to help locals understand the creek with the hope of eventually restoring it. *Art as Environment—A Cultural Action at the Plum Tree Creek,* with Bamboo Curtain Studio, began a multi-year, interdisciplinary arts project.

The Plum Tree Creek flows 12 kilometres from Datun Mountain through agricultural and residential areas of Zhuwei, then into the Danshui River. As Zhuwei developed into a commuter town of Taipei and increased in population and density, the creek suffered. Once used for cooking, washing and swimming, it became polluted from industrial and agricultural waste and residential sewage. Flooding was also a problem, caused by the manipulation of the creek's path through 'concrete channels, culverts, a major freeway, and metro lines' (Goto et al. 2014). Covering the creek in favour of urban expansion – to

---

[7] This follows Mandarin naming conventions of surname followed by first name.

facilitate more roads and infrastructure – is based on the idea that urban life is not compatible with 'nature', furthering the urban/nature division. Wu's cultural action for Plum Tree Creek demonstrated bio-urban concepts through its recognition and advocacy of the multitude of vibrant ecological relationships that make up urban life and the view that re-engaging with them increases the quality of urban living. The project used arts interventions to engage a variety of community members in a form of 'daylighting' the creek (restoring and uncovering often buried or forgotten waterways).

The National Culture and Arts Foundation in Taiwan funded the Plum Tree Creek project (2011–2013). It grew to involve 'a series of cultural actions from over 60 local and international artists, curators, professionals and NGOs intersecting multiple stakeholders. We have now reached more than 80,000 participants' (Bamboo Curtain Studio 2022). In 2013, the project won the Taishin Arts Award, one of Taiwan's most prestigious arts and culture awards. Bamboo Curtain Studio, an NGO, operated an international artist residency programme from their site close to the Plum Tree Creek in Zhuwei from 2009 until about 2020. This provided an opportunity for other artists to continue to engage with the Plum Tree Creek after the initial phase of the project ended.

Art as Environment—A Cultural Action at the Plum Tree Creek had multiple strands (and a variety of sub-strands). There was an eco-education and future classroom strand organised by artist Margaret Shiu (founder of Bamboo Curtain Studio). A team worked across three schools to facilitate different programmes to engage school children in thinking about the creek. This included what they called a community theatre intervention. This involved collecting stories from a group of semi-retired women who lived around the creek and then using those stories to create a piece of theatre which was performed back to them by local school children, bridging generations. The memories and experiences of the Plum Tree Creek from the women connected the school children to the creek in different ways, allowing them to imagine and perform an alternative relationship to the creek other than it being invisible and/or ignored. Another aspect of this strand was a year-long project with Zhuwei Elementary School and Shiu called 'There Is a Creek in Front of My School Gate'. This involved taking the students on field trips along the creek, from the area of the creek that still had agriculture on its shores to the more densely populated areas with the polluted creek closer to the school. The students recorded their experiences through art activities and then created a graduation show based on them. Local authorities were invited to the graduation show, and according to Shiu, they were moved enough to promise to make a change leading to the restoration of the creek (Goto et al. 2014).

Another strand of the Plum Tree Creek cultural action was a food project. Monthly community meals, usually breakfast, based on locally-grown, seasonal food, were offered at the events to bring together local community members with different professionals and experts to generate discussion about the creek and local life. Resonating with Bennett's idea of food as an operator of wide-ranging ecological relationships (2010), Wu used food as a starting point for wider discussions of conservation, urban planning, community use and sustainable agriculture.

Wu is a pioneer of socially-engaged arts practice in Taiwan and wanted to bring her work to the ecological context of Zhuwei. She thought that if the residents accepted the polluted state of the creek, it would lead to forgetting its previous use and role in community life, ultimately diminishing the possibilities of future ways of living around the creek. Creating arts interventions that allowed community members to have conversations and creatively explore the river and their experience was important for Wu. One aim of the project was to use the area as a micro example of urban living. As Bamboo Curtain Studio states, 'We hope to establish the surrounding area of Plum Tree Creek into a micro-prototype of a liveable city that integrates ecology and creativity' (Bamboo Curtain Studio 2018). The liveable city is one that is accessible, equitable, often walkable and has abundant public green spaces, acknowledging that it is part of 'nature' and building it with that recognition. For Wu, this aim was achieved as the community started to use and pay attention to the creek and the local government was engaged. This was one of the lasting effects of the project on the city:

> The Plum Tree Creek project generated visible changes. New Taipei City government started to pay more attention to this waterway, and is now working on a new landscape plan. Previously they never discussed policy plans with local residents; now they send the plans to us, and we then, through Bamboo Curtain Studio, distribute the plans in the community. A platform for dialogue has been established. (Wu in Bo 2016: 160).

Conscious, creative and careful urban planning is needed to create sustainable and equitable cities. The Plum Tree Creek project was able to facilitate community participation in urban planning through engagement in arts and performance.

New Taipei City is different from the two American cities analysed in the first half of this section. Where there is cheaper fuel, cities tend to be more spread out and sprawling (such as in North America). Where fuel is more expensive, cities are denser, usually with public transportation infrastructure, as the cost of running private vehicles may be prohibitive for much of the population. New

Taipei City underwent rapid urban development as people who worked in Taipei needed a nearby location to live. It developed as a commuter city, increasing rapidly in popularity, particularly after the building of the MRT metro line in 1997. Older buildings were replaced with high-rise apartments to accommodate the growth. The agriculture of the area (cultivated particularly during the Japanese occupation between 1895 and 1945) gave way to large-scale residential and commercial developments, changing and contaminating the creek as a result.

The Plum Tree Creek project sees the city as part of nature and hopes to draw out new ways of living in a city that acknowledges and supports the varied ecological relationships within it. For Wu, the focus on the micro area of the creek allowed for a local focus and change:

> Our work is to excavate the complex issues underlying the specific problems of this small creek, including the way we think about development, the way we imagine land. A single art action will not be able to resolve the predicament, but it can energize more people to start thinking about it. Social change always starts with alternative social imaginaries. (Wu in Bo 2016: 163).

The cultural actions that were part of the Plum Tree Creek project were akin to what Courtney Ryan calls urban micro-performances, in which local practices playfully traverse vegetal and human life as 'spatialized eco-performance' (2023: 9). She writes that these small acts can, at times, create cracks in the normalisation of crisis (environmental and social) to reveal the interconnectivity and shared vulnerability of humans and more-than-human nature. Although the actions of the Plum Tree Creek project were micro and localised, and as Wu articulates, will not solve the predicament, they revealed the way in which the creek influences urban living in the area and invited people to see the creek differently. For Wu, this was the first step in creating more liveable cities.

Not only is the city alive with a multitude of human and more-than-human ecological relationships, it is also haunted by historical and continuing injustices. The colonial history of Taiwan has influenced and shaped its cities. For Tomonori Sugimoto, a researcher working on Indigenous rights in Taiwan, 'The city and Indigeneity are seen as contradictory' (Sugimoto 2023: 130). This is despite the urbanisation of Indigenous peoples in Taiwan, with large populations living in cities, mostly due to land dispossession and a decline in agricultural production (Sugimoto 2023: 130). After successive colonialisation from the Dutch, Spanish, the Koxinga, the Qing, Han Chinese, Japanese rule and the Republic of China exile government, Sugimoto identifies Taipei as a city on stolen Indigenous land: 'what is known today as Taipei is a territory of the Indigenous Ketagalan tribe' (131). He further argues that, excluding a few monuments, 'the original occupation of Taipei by the Ketagalan is completely forgotten, just as residents of cities such as New York and San Francisco rarely think about these cities' Indigenous residents.' (131). Even though the city is home to tens of thousands of Indigenous peoples and communities 'many Indigenous and non-Indigenous people continue to characterise Taipei as a place of Indigenous absence, a site of loss for Indigenous culture and authenticity.' (130–131). Accordingly, this lack of visibility calls for a decolonial approach to urban development and organisation to acknowledge Indigenous ways of relating to the land.

Taiwan's Indigenous people's spatialised urban performances illustrate the way in which Indigeneity relates to urban spaces. Sugimoto describes these interventions as:

> Indigeneity, as happens when Pangcah/Amis people forage in Taipei's riverside parks, grow their favourite plants under freeway overpasses, hold harvest festivals in parking lots, create hubs on urban streets and corners and refuse to leave public lands where they have established communities. Through such practices, they are reimagining the relationship between Indigeneity and the city and (re)inscribing Indigeneity into the urban fabric of Taipei. (Sugimoto 2023: 134)

Here, Indigeneity operates as a set of practices, skills and orientations grounded in Indigenous epistemologies and ontologies that can be transported to (now) urban geographies and ecologies. They offer a decolonial approach to the conceptualisation of cities, 'they unsettle settler-determined hegemonic courses of urban development, [and] the logics of private property that enclose and exclude people', reminding settlers that all land, no matter the current development, is Indigenous land (Sugimoto 2023: 134). Urban development and the overlooking of Indigenous practices in Taiwan mirror London's colonial structures, as Peter Morin's work (detailed below) shows.

Cultural Graffiti in London

2013. Buckingham Palace. Tahltan Nation artist Peter Morin has travelled here from what is now known as Canada to undertake a series of 14 performance inventions at historical sites and monuments across the city. At Buckingham Palace, he is wearing a black and red blanket, with white buttons stitched to form a pattern of a crow wearing armour, in a traditional Tahltan style. He is also wearing handmade high-top moccasins (or hunter moccasins) made by his Aunty Lilly. For this intervention, he wears a black domino mask in the style of the Lone Ranger that includes hand-sewn mother-of-pearl buttons to match his button blanket. He sets himself up directly in front of the gates at

Buckingham Palace, he sings directly into the ground underneath their palace, he sings and drums around their monument directly in front of their palace; and when done, he walks over to their gate and marks their gate with these words: 'today you lose everything, today you lose everything, because we remain, we are vibrant, we are Idle No More'. Afterwards, outside Canada Gate, he sings Tahltan songs directly to stones underfoot, to the monuments, to his ancestors – past, present and emerging. For this entire performance, he plays a drum with the words 'this drum supports Indigenous voice' as he sings. He is accompanied by a documentation team of witnesses and surrounded by sometimes curious tourists. After marking the Buckingham Palace gate, he turns to walk away from the palace. A police officer stops him to interrogate his previous actions, but the officer is eventually satisfied with the explanation of Morin being a university researcher who is researching the effect of British colonialism on Indigenous bodies. He does not detain him. Morin sings at other monuments across Greater London, including sites with explicit Indigenous connections, such as Pocahontas' gravesite at St George's Church, Gravesend, and Mungo Martin's Totem Pole (that was carved in Canada, after the Potlatch ban was lifted in 1953 as a gift to Queen Elizabeth) that now resides in Great Windsor Park.

The bio-urban considers the living relationships that make up cities and how different performances can reveal and nurture them. These living relationships also include the residue of colonialism, the ghosts or presence of colonial legacies of violence that are embedded in monuments and statues. Colonialism shaped the living relationships of the city and continues to exert ideological control. Historian Coll-Peter Thrush asserts that Indigenous people's presence in London is not 'hidden histories' but forced forgetting (2016). In fact, when Indigenous visitors/captives or diplomats from North America, New Zealand/Aotearoa and Australia were in London, they were hyper-visible because of their difference. Treated as curiosities, performers, 'noble savages' and/or slaves, Thrush contends they were some of the most visible people in London between the sixteenth and twentieth centuries. Morin, dressed in Tahltan traditional dress, was hyper-visible during his performance acts, inciting curiosity as well as suspicion (including a police confrontation). The sonic/aural graffiti performed by Morin was delivered to more-than-human actants, but it was necessary to negotiate London as a highly surveilled and demarcated space. The commissioners of the work, theatre scholars Helen Gilbert and Dani Phillipson, write that 'while the main "audience" for these performances was the site of the song – the ground, the stones, the artwork, the traces of ancestors remaining – Morin felt it was important to include witnesses to his work. The immediate role of these individuals was to document the performances and support the artist by negotiating the everyday practical challenges of working in London's public spaces' (Gilbert and Phillipson 2015: 15). While performing, Morin overhead observers at these busy tourist sites say 'I think he thinks he's an Indian' and 'shhh ... this is an Indigenous performance' (Morin in Robinson 2019: 229). For Indigenous sound scholar Dylan Robinson (Stó:lō/Skwah), who was documenting the work, Morin was enacting Indigenous healing, sovereignty and kinship through his performance. Although this was not necessarily readable to the public of tourists visiting the sites and monuments, because of the lack of visible colonial and Indigenous histories.

Morin is an artist, curator and professor at the Ontario College of Art and Design, Toronto. Morin's *Cultural Graffiti in London* was commissioned as part of the Indigeneity in the Contemporary World Research project, funded by the European Research Council from 2009 to 2014, led by Helen Gilbert. Gilbert and Phillipson commissioned it for the international exhibition of Indigenous arts and performance, *Ecocentrix: Indigenous Arts, Sustainable Acts* in London. For the commission, they 'began to imagine how indigenous encounters with/in London, past, present and future, might be embedded in the city's artistic substrate' (Gilbert and Phillipson 2015: 7). The resulting commission of *Cultural Graffiti* spoke directly to the land and built environment of colonial London. Morin describes his cultural graffiti, singing the songs of the Tahltan Nation where the monuments meet the land, 'as a way of embodying Tahltan knowledge, embodying a way of being in relation to people, way of being in relation to the land here ... trying to enact a direct challenge to the colonial power' (Morin in Huarcaya and Phillipson 2013). It was developed from his long-term interest in how performance and Tahltan ceremonial practices might interact (Robinson 2019: 224). Morin, in a mac jacket and a beaded hide vest made by Tahltan artist Penny Louie, sings Tahltan Songs composed by Tahltan Elder Beal Carlick at historical monuments and places around the city: British landmarks, including the Houses of Parliament, Buckingham Palace, and Big Ben; Indigenous monuments such as Pocahontas' gravesite and Kwakwaka'wakw carver Mungo Martin's Totem Pole in Great Windsor Park, Southwark Cathedral; and contemporary pilgrimage sites like the Princess Diana Memorial Fountain in Hyde Park and a Banksy in Brixton. Here, Indigeneity is a transportable concept, which can be enacted as a way of thinking and a set of practices, in different geographies and urban centres. Morin's singing takes on a different meaning depending on the site: at the landmark sites, it calls forth a buried Indigenous presence erased in the monuments of empire. At the Indigenous sites, he sings in solidarity and kinship. Indigeneity is enacted through singing and ceremony, speaking to ancestors past, present and emerging, cutting through the colonial legacy of Indigenous erasure in London.

The work is identified by Gilbert and Phillipson as a 'sonic rebellion against the hegemonic exercise of colonial power [which] involved an assertion of cultural resilience that often ended with the statement, "we are still here"' (2015: 10). I want to extend this analysis by suggesting that it draws out the ecology of the city, past, present and future by acknowledging colonialism as the root of climate crisis. By calling ancestors through sonic graffiti and the phrase 'we are still here' there is an implication through the sonic graffiti tag that the ancestors will continue to be here in the future. The tagging marks the city sites with Indigenous presence and resists a history of forgetting through a vibrant materiality. This tagging provokes questions that interrogate what it means to acknowledge, name and properly reconcile the violence of colonialism in the UK. There has been no truth and reconciliation process undertaken in the UK. Writer and law lecturer Kojo Koram has called for one in a 2020 article for *The Guardian* saying 'The prevailing attitude we hold to our imperial history is one of ignorance and complacency: the British empire is something that we should be proud of, but not pay any great attention to. It should be admired but remain unexamined – the mood music of the British psyche, rather than a cause of current events.' (Koram 2020). Morin's sonic graffiti plays in reaction to this mood music, calling it to the foreground. Koram goes on to call for a Truth and Reconciliation process, that asks broad questions about how the UK has profited from Empire, which is needed if the UK is ever going to meaningfully grapple with its systemic inequalities. He writes: 'it's only by unpicking the legacy of empire that we will have a chance to really think about the type of Britain we want to build today' (Koram 2020). Morin's work uses Indigenous terms and Tahltan cultural practices to address the ignorance and complacency of the UK in ongoing colonialist effects.

There was a particularly striking example of a moment in the Ecocentrix exhibition that displayed the forgetting and invisibility of Indigenous histories and presence in London. It was when two visitors were watching the video documentation of Morin's performance in Windsor at the Kwakwaka'wakw totem pole. Gilbert and Phillipson write about this moment as exemplifying Indigenous erasure:

> two visitors, intrigued by the video's inclusion in the exhibit were surprised to learn that the Kwakwaka'wakw totem pole featuring as the site/audience of Morin's song rested in Great Windsor Park just outside London, not

"somewhere in America". Indigenous peoples had not figured in their previous understandings of the city's history, neither in terms of trade, migration routes, diplomacy nor art. (Gilbert and Phillipson 2015: 29)

Morin's work brings Indigenous art, awareness and practices into the city where Indigenous presences have been wilfully forgotten or erased. It injects urban ecologies with a sense of how colonialism patterns cities, often through Indigenous marginalisation.

Marking Indigenous historical, current and future presence in the city through art offers potential for reshaping harmful colonial systems which underpin both social inequalities and the climate crisis. Morin's performance centres Indigenous worldviews. Algonquin theatre maker Yvette Nolan writes of Indigenous theatre being used to make medicine, which builds community, negotiates solidarity and performs acts of remembering (2015: 3). Morin's work builds community with both ancestors and the more-than-human actants in urban spaces while performing acts of remembering. Morin makes these links when reflecting on his cultural graffiti intervention at the Tower of London, he says:

> The tower of London was a dream. understanding how the crown jewels and the monarchy influence Indigenous ways of knowing, it's all a dream until you stand, actually stand there and sing. ... and singing the song is also acknowledging this bloody history, and also resource extraction, this creation of this place. (Morin quoted in Gilbert and Phillipson 2015: 10)

Morin makes connections between 'bloody' history and resource extraction to the influence on, and presumed suppression of, Indigenous ways of knowing. The colonial project and ideology of empire have ongoing effects in what is now known as Canada and Tāłtān Konelīne (Tahltan) territory in northern British Columbia. Colonial ideology has shaped Indigenous experience, marginalisation and violence by the state in Canada, including suppression of Indigenous rights, the violence of residential schools and management and use of lands and waterways. The Crown Jewels in the Tower of London are materially connected, through violence and extraction, to Indigenous experience in Canada (and other 'commonwealth' nations who endured British colonialism). The places that Morin 'tags' in the colonial metropolis of London are imbued with agentic cultural graffiti that marks the ongoing colonial project, resisting Indigenous erasure and hopefully reshaping relationships between people and land in light of the climate crisis.

London is a haunted landscape. It is haunted by the colonial (and ecological) violence that built the city, restyled in the neo-liberal fashion of a modern, cosmopolitan city. Tsing et al. conceptualise the haunting of the Anthropocene, writing that 'the winds of the Anthropocene carry ghosts – the vestiges and signs of past ways of life still charged in the present ... Our ghosts are the traces of the more-than-human histories through which ecologies are made and unmade' (Tsing et al. 2017: 1). *Cultural Graffiti* calls forth those traces of more-than-human histories of the landscapes and monuments that hold colonial vestiges and residues. The willful or enforced 'forgetting' of the violence of colonialism shapes London as a landscape, including its monuments and tourist sites: 'Forgetting, in itself, remakes landscapes, as we privilege some assemblages over others. Yet ghosts remind us. Ghosts point to our forgetting, showing us how living landscapes reimbued with earlier tracks and traces' (Tsing et al. 2017: 6). Resisting the pressure to forget, this work engages in a remembering of the colonial and ecological violence that lies as an invisible layer blanketing the city. Morin's sonic tags call forth these human and more-than-human ghosts with the words 'we are still here'.

Morin's performance makes visible the Indigenous presence haunting London's colonial cityscape. He sings and speaks to the foundations of empire through the literal foundation of the monuments that represent it: the bricks beneath Buckingham Palace, for example, or the foundations of the statue of Queen Victoria at Royal Holloway University. Morin wanted the stones that hold up this colonial empire to know that Indigenous people are still here, these songs were also reminders that these ancient relationships are important. Through his performance, Morin not only locates Indigenous presence in the bricks, ground and structures of the city, he also gestures towards the building of these monuments by forgotten or invisible labour. The ghosts of this invisible labour and capital gained through the exploitation and enslavement of humans and more-than-humans are gestured to in Morin's performance. These are spectres of Indigenous presence and ancestors Morin is directly speaking to.

The city of London is built on a colonialist sense of time that values progress at all costs and selective forgetting. Morin's work ruptures this sense of time by focusing on pasts, presents and yet-to-come descedents of Indigenous peoples and their presence imprinted on the landscape. Morin sings directly to the material and ideological foundations of colonialism, saying 'we are alive'. Countering the colonial urge to manage, extract and commodify, Morin's work punctures the vision of progress put forth by the monuments of London. Morin's work encourages witnessing some uncomfortable truths about the wealth and progress of London and the 'bloody' impact of its role as a world city. London's imperial impact on contemporary global politics (particularly around oil extraction and trade) is examined in Section Two.

Despite living in an age of ecological crisis, the above works represent small revolutions in coexistence, radical examples of the way we can reclaim the city, making it more equitable, pleasurable and just. They all enact the concept of the bio-urban through revealing the aliveness of the city. This aliveness, containing the entanglement of human and more-than-human 'nature', is fractured and uneven, containing systemic inequalities, exacerbated by urban development. A farm run by artists under a highway overpass in a high-need neighbourhood in San Francisco demonstrates the way in which art interventions with more-than-human co-performers can disrupt the urban/nature dialectic, offering alternative and more just ways of organising urban living. Garbage trucks and waste processing sites in New York City reveal the invisible and underappreciated job of keeping New York alive while highlighting the environmental injustice of locating these sites in neighbours with less social capital. Spatialised, local micro-performances in Taiwan engaged urban inhabitants, renewing a seemingly lost ecological relationship with Plum Tree Creek and influencing new urban development processes. Cities marked by colonialism, such as London, are haunted by Indigenous pasts, presents and futures, marked by Morin's singing of the Tahltan Nation's anthem to the foundations of empire enacting Indigenous sovereignty and kinship. These works express the aliveness of the city in multiple ways and iterations through transient or temporary encounters of urban eco-performances.

2 Petro-cities

The Museum of English Rural Life (MERL) in Reading, UK, displays a slightly surprising object: a bright white glass shell globe, emblazoned with 'Shellmex' in red letters. It is from the top of a 1950s petrol pump, and it is housed in a glass cabinet full of objects in the shop/café area of the museum. The recognition of the part petrol plays in English rural life makes the object of interest in the collection. There is small black writing around the base that says: 'Property of Shell-Mex & BP ltd'. Shell-Mex and BP were the result of a merger of the UK marketing operations of Royal Dutch Shell (known as Shell) and British Petroleum (BP) from the 1930s to the 1970s. Shell itself started as an antiques company in London in the 1830s, whose business included importing and selling seashells. The Samuel brothers expanded their father's antique business into the Shell Transport and Trading company, importing and exporting goods from Asia and the Middle East. The company merged with Royal Dutch Petroleum in 1907 to become Shell, one of the largest oil corporations, shaping global contemporary socio-ecological relationships.

The yellow shell logo is now an ubiquitous brand identity, hailing drivers on the motorway. It is the subject of protest signs, signalling the dirty deeds of oil extraction across the globe. The Shellmex globe at MERL memorialises the oil and petrol we rely on every day and the global movement of capital, people, resources and more-than-human ecologies that drive oil extraction, production and transportation. Filling up a car with petrol, perhaps at a Shell station, is a local action with global reverberations. This action, and our regular consumption of petroleum-based plastic products, connects us to global ecological relationships and complex power structures and systems, founded on colonialism. This substance has an outsized material impact on world ecologies. The film *Mad Max: Fury Road* (2014) fittingly calls it 'guzzoline', a portmanteau combining gasoline and guzzle (and highlighting reliance on gas-guzzling vehicles), which typifies petrol use in contemporary life. The Shellmex sign is the visible starting point that connects oil extraction in Nigeria to urban life in Britain. The performance works in this section all make visible a material relationship to oil and its environmental injustices, which are often obscured in Western consumer relations.

This section focuses on petro-cities, and the way in which the power formations of global cities (such as London) shape the commodity of oil and impact much smaller cities such as Calgary, Alberta, Canada and Port Harcourt, Rivers State, Nigeria. The idea of the bio-urban is nuanced by recognising the complex interplay between the power formations of a city and the global ecological consequences. The cities of the Global North have far-reaching and devastating effects on cities and places in the Global South, through the material connection to oil. According to geographer Doreen Massey, London (and more specifically the City as the financial centre) is at the centre of neoliberalism, and 'is a command centre, place of orchestration, and significant beneficiary of its continuing operation. This city stands, then, as a crucial node in the production of what is an increasingly unequal world' (Massey 2011: 8). London is a centre of power for things like deregulation, a crucial node that allows oil extraction to continue unfettered despite the environmental injustices and human rights abuses.

Naomi Klein characterises these connections as an invisible seesaw of oil relations: 'Alberta and Iraq have been connected to each other through a kind of invisible seesaw: As Baghdad burns, destabilizing the entire region and sending oil prices soaring, Calgary booms' (Klein 2007: n.p.). The invisible seesaw that connects petro-city Calgary, Alberta (home of tar sands oil operations) with Baghdad, Iraq, is more of an invisible interconnected web that links petrol-guzzling consumption with Indigenous land dispossession, war, conflict, environmental pollution, sacrificial species and people in all oil-producing regions. War in Baghdad destabilises the oil supply of the region, and the gap is filled by the Alberta tar sands. Through climate change, these connections become more evident and fatal. The performances in this section aim to make visible this seesaw or web that connects global urban centres such as London with devastating effects in the Global South. This section follows oil as a commodity and traces its impact on social, ecological and political structures, with the city as the centre of power.

Following the global community of oil, this section starts in London, a global financial centre which includes the headquarters of Shell, before moving to the Niger Delta, Nigeria, to consider the local impacts of oil extraction and then finally concluding back in London as experienced by a British-born member of the Nigerian diaspora. It focuses on the ecological relationships between oil extraction and the capitalist drive that perpetuates the attendant violence. *Oil City (2013)* was a site-specific immersive piece by Platform, taking place in and around London's City distinct, merging fictional characters with real locations in a story about the very real ecologically devastating but financially rewarding Alberta tar sands. After tracing the money funding these oil operations, the focus moves to the site of oil extraction in the Niger Delta. In Port Harcourt, Nigeria, Bright Ugochukwu Eke's work captures some of the effects of oil extraction on water, tracing the links from air and water pollution to the impact on humans in the 'sacrifice zones' (particularly marginalised peoples in the Niger Delta whose land and health are considered disposable in order to maintain oil operations). The section moves back to London and concludes with the story of Nigerian diaspora and climate activism in Britain today, making links between British colonialism and climate crisis through Fehinti Balogun's lived experience in *Can I Live?* (2021).

Considering these three pieces together allows us to trace the impact of oil extraction, making visible the material and environmental impact. Scholars Balkan and Nandi write about the 'present absence' (after Fredric Jameson) of oil in the American (and British) imagination: 'essentially the constitutive outside that has long forged the colonial elsewheres of our imperial imaginary—oil has effectively resisted representation owing to both a conscious refusal to acknowledge the human and environmental costs of its extraction as well as the aforementioned spatial amnesia, which renders such sites invisible' (Balkan and Nandi 2021: 2). The performances in this section aim to make visible the 'present absence' of oil extraction: powerful global cities that finance and control it as well as the Global South cities that suffer the violence as a consequence of extraction, the relationship between oil producers and oil consumers. Following Balkan and Nandi, although not fictions, the performances each do something similar: 'Oil fictions foreground invisibility, itinerancy, and precarity, materializing invisibility through their scrutiny of the uneven terrain of our global petrosphere' (Balkan and Nandi 2021: 6). By foregrounding and materialising the invisibility and precarity of oil relations, each performance work opens up a different aspect oil extraction, drawing out the environmental and more-than-human injustices it entails.

Oil City

I book a ticket for a performance at ArtsAdmin in London for the Two Degrees Festival on climate without knowing much about it. A day before the scheduled performance, I receive a cryptic email from 'The Lawyer' with some instructions:

> Dear all
>
> Looking forward to seeing you tomorrow. It's an absolute pleasure to have your assistance. Couple of thoughts before we meet . . .
>
> I'd recommend you wear comfortable shoes for our trip – but keep them smart mind. On which note, ideally you'd be dressed to impress, business interview attire I suppose. It's probably best if we blend in, as I'm sure you'll understand.
>
> And keep your wits about you while we're out – look both ways before crossing the road and so on!
>
> And let me say now thanks for agreeing to meet with me – the more people I speak to, the more it seems like we're going to see movement on this thing. Fills me with optimism about the whole situation out there. I was reading up on the case law until the small hours last night. If anyone can get something to move us forward on this, it's you.
>
> See you in the Toynbee studios cafe – you'll find me beside the black flowers.
>
> Yours, ever hopeful,
>
> The Lawyer' (Evans and Platform 2013)

I go to the café at the designated time and find the table with black flowers and a small group of other slightly confused audience members. The Lawyer (played by Nick Underwood) greets us and thanks us for coming to help him out with his case. We then follow him out to his car in the car park behind the theatre, where he gives us smart clothing to borrow (if required) in order to fit in with the City crowd. We are then driven a few blocks down the road and dropped off at Liverpool Street Station and told to meet a journalist who has some damning information about a bank's involvement with oil companies and the tar sands development in Alberta, Canada. The Journalist (played by Rebecca Omogbehin) is expecting us and beckons us over while on the phone to her editor in what sounds like a heated conversation. We stand inside the busy station, leaning in to listen to The Journalist as people shuffle around us. She tells us about a whistleblower contact that has incriminating information about the financing of the tar sands. She shows us a document of notes from a meeting between then UK Prime Minister David Cameron and then Canadian Prime Minister Stephen Harper about selling tar sands oil to the European Union. There was talk of the EU banning imports from the tar sands because of how 'dirty' the oil operation is. Since UK corporations finance it and stand to profit from it, they opposed this ban. (The EU voted against this ban as well as additional labelling for tar sands oil as 'highly polluting' in 2014). We meet the Whistleblower source (played by Natalie De Luna), in another corner of the station, and we gather around a small speaker connected to a mobile phone to hear a recording of bankers. She tasks us with meeting up with an Indigenous activist from Alberta to hand over some documents that evidence corruption and wrongdoing. We are then told to meet with a cleaner to hear the damaging information they have. As we continue to meet up with clandestine characters (all played by the same three actors), eavesdrop on conversations and follow key players, a picture of a large-scale conspiracy (or perhaps collusion) begins to unfold about the potentially illegal development of very dirty tar sands. There is a race against the clock to get enough information to publish a story in a national newspaper. All of this takes place in the Broadgate development of The City of London, home to some of the biggest banks in the world. *Oil City* (written by Mel Evans, directed by Sam Rowe) asks critical questions about how the tar sands development was funded, who is profiting and who is losing.

The site-based performance was produced by Platform, an arts, activism, education and research organisation. They are focused on the social and ecological impact of the oil industry and have developed projects to oppose oil companies funding the arts (Art Not Oil coalition), oil funding of universities (Knowledge and Power – Fossil Fuel Universities report), and an audio tour of the Tate Britain and Tate Modern, *Tate à Tate*, highlighting and advocating for an end of their BP sponsorship (with Liberate Tate). They blend in-depth, investigative research with performance and community projects to reveal hidden relationships and commodity chains that are shaping the social and ecological world.

Oil City reveals global ecological relationships within local places. The piece was site-specific and immersive, taking place in London's financial district, and weaving together fictional characters with actual locations to explore the story of the Alberta tar sands, its ecological damage and financial rewards. The tar sands development is the world's third largest supply of oil, and through its ferocious consumption of resources, deforestation and the carbon emissions from oil extraction, it is one of the worst environmental projects in the world and is quickly becoming Canada's largest source of carbon emissions (Grant et al. 2013). Tar sands oil uses open-pit mining and is therefore much more water and energy-intensive to extract than other forms of oil. There have also been several toxic leaks from the tailing ponds that are needed for the waste runoff.

The Activist character (played by Natalie De Luna) tells the audience her grandmother is from the Athabasca Chipewyan First Nations, and that is how she knows about the situation of Indigenous peoples in the 'sacrifice zone' of the tar sands. The 'sacrifice zone' is an area surrounding the tar sands that is deemed acceptable to sacrifice – the land and the people living there – in order to support the oil operations. The Activist tells us there are many First Nations being affected by the 'dirty' tar sands extraction, with soaring cancer rates and environmental devastation. The Activist explains that water is sacred to these Indigenous communities, and this is how they communicate stories. They cannot simply 'relocate' as the oil companies would like them to because of the ancestral, spiritual and material connection to the land and water. The Activist shows us a copy of Treaty 8, signed by Queen Victoria, that is ostensibly meant to govern the land around the tar sands. It states that the Indigenous nations of the area have the right to pursue their vocational land and water uses, such as hunting, fishing, etc, exempting the area from interference and development by the Crown. She argues that companies such as Shell and BP are infringing upon these rights when the water and land are being polluted from oil extraction, and therefore preventing the vocational (and traditional) use.

The Cleaner for the offices of Royal Bank of Scotland (RBS) hands the audience a document that shows RBS and BP admitting that they did not have the fair and free consent of all the Indigenous peoples in the area of the tar sands, despite requiring that for the development to happen. Agreements with Indigenous nations and communities in the tar sands have been controversial, with some court cases brought by Indigenous groups against the Canadian government for infringing on treaty rights. Indigenous scholar Glen Coulthard (Dene) writes that Canada is similar to other settler-colonial states in their foundational colonialist structures to Indigenous rights, including land and water. He writes:

> in the Canadian context, colonial domination continues to be structurally committed to maintain— through force, fraud, and more recently, so-called "negotiations"— ongoing state access to the land and resources that contradictorily provide the material and spiritual sustenance of Indigenous societies on the one hand, and the foundation of colonial state-formation, settlement, and capitalist development on the other. (2014: 7)

This colonial state formation continues in London, where RBS and BP reap the profits of damaging the land and water of Indigenous territories. For Native Studies scholar Patricia McCormack, it is important to remember: 'Aboriginal people have occupied northern Alberta since the end of the last ice age ... they are immersed in and "read" the land as places with multiple cultural meanings, which in turn helped shape their cultures and identities' (2017: 110). The settler state does not recognise the way in which Indigenous peoples relate to the land, water and related kin that reside there. Imposing settler colonialist values (such as that land is a resource for capitalist gain) results in further marginalisation of Indigenous rights in Canada.

The Indigenous activist movement, Idle No More, was started in response to tar sands extraction. Then, Canadian Prime Minister Stephen Harper passed a bill to remove environmental 'obstacles' to development projects, effectively making the expansion of the tar sands extraction project easier. Using large-scale participatory actions (such as circle dances in shopping centres) and utilising media attention, Idle No More was able to mobilise Indigenous people and allies across Canada against the bill (although ultimately Harper did not concede). Idle No More, as I have written about elsewhere, was a touch point for Indigenous activist resurgence and environmental justice in Canada (Woynarski 2020a). From an intersectional ecological perspective, there is also a link to gender-based violence that haunts Indigenous communities, and the proximity to male-dominated oil extraction sites contributes to the Missing and Murdered Indigenous Women crisis.

The interactive form of *Oil City* blurred the line between reality and fiction. The specifics of the performance were fictional, but the political context, locations and the major players (Royal Bank of Scotland, BP the Canadian and UK government) are still real in 2024. The audience talked to, followed and spied on actors around the City, surrounded by actual City workers such as bankers, lawyers and journalists. At one point, The Activist leads the audience past the RBS offices and points out that this was the place where the tar sands deal was signed. Theatre scholar Stephen Scott-Bottoms writes about this layering of fact and fiction in the performance: 'The City becomes a strangely heightened, theatrical space (which it already is, of course, in many respects!), and everyone in it becomes part of the intrigue' (Scott-Bottoms 2013). This blurring or layering of theatrical fiction with reality allowed the audience to access and engage with the complexities of tracing the money in the oil commodity chain.

London, as a world city, is in a particularly unique position in relation to global ecological relations. In *World City* (2011), Massey argues that in a global city such as London, 'there is a vast geography of dependencies, relations and effects that spreads out from here around the globe' (13), making London a nucleus of ecological and material influences and exchanges. She also points out that world cities are vital to neoliberal globalisation, reflecting market formations (such as wealth inequality). These neoliberal formations influence global relationships and bear ecological responsibility for the far-reaching effects of material lifestyles. Massey points out: 'In obvious material terms London's existence depends on daily supplies from around the planet and, at the other end of the process as it were – its production of waste, its emission of carbon – its footprint is also geographically extensive' (181). In addition to the daily resources consumed and the waste produced in London, its impact as a world city extends to the less visible political and financial power structures. *Oil City* dissected only a few of these ecological effects that spread out from London, but highlighted the influence of the 'world city' and the neoliberal market forces that govern it.

London is also a petro-city, not because it produces oil but rather because it finances its production. As Massey notes, 'together oil and gas account in one way or another for about a quarter of London's stock exchange; Shell and BP have major offices and headquarters in London; London is utterly dependent on oil' (2011: 201). Platform has traced the connections between London and global oil extraction in what they call The Carbon Web. 'Oil runs through every sector of society. London, our city, is one of the global centres of the oil industry. Oil companies use the city to extract a combination of financial, political, legal and technological services that enable them to produce, pump, transport, refine and sell oil and gas.' (Platform 2024). As part of The Carbon Web project, Platform traced all the mechanisms of financial, political, legal and technological apparatuses that facilitate the extraction of oil by Shell and BP through London. In *Oil City*, parts of the carbon web are dramatised through a specific context of financing the Alberta tar sands.

During an informal chat after the performance, my fellow audience members said that the interactive structure made them much more engrossed in the issues of the piece. Not only did it raise awareness about the way oil is being extracted at great ecological expense, but the performance also provided an embodied experience of the story in a way no news article could. The performance took a seemingly foreign problem and revealed the UK's involvement, compliance and profits. The Canadian activist told the audience a very personal story about the significance of the land of the tar sands to First Nations people of the area, which was commented on as being a side of the story not heard much, especially in the UK media. Sarah Ann Standing (2012) identifies this as an aesthetic of eco-activist performance, 'bringing the remote close' (153) or making visible and giving voice to things broadly considered foreign or remote. She writes that performance can draw out the global impacts of local practices. My fellow audience members said they would be interested in following the real story of the tar sands after the performance, as they felt they were now engaged in it.

This is in part because of the immersive experience of re-imagining the city, which foregrounded ecological relationships and exposed the connectedness of seemingly foreign environments.

Oil City fosters bio-urban thinking by revealing global, interconnected ecological-political-social relationships. The experience of performance helps us see the city as part of a larger mesh of connections, in which everyday urban processes have global, and often destructive, reverberations.

Acid Rain and Shields

From London, I now trace the oil commodity chain to one of its extraction points in the Niger Delta, through installations and performances that reveal the devastating consequences of this colonialist-driven extraction.

Acid Rain (2006) is an installation that features large, suspended water droplets that form a pattern of falling rain. It is acidified water (formed through contamination from battery acid) in a transparent plastic film. These large acid water droplets are suspended from above in an outdoor installation. The piece focuses on contaminated drinking water in Nigeria caused by petrol refineries. Water molecules dissolve the effluents (waste and pollution) and return to the earth in the form of acid rain. This acid rain causes deforestation and impacts drinking water in the Niger Delta. *Acid Rain* is by Bright Ugochukwu Eke, a noted Nigerian artist who has presented work internationally, including representing Nigeria at the Venice Biennale 2015. His work reveals the way in which the violent oil extraction in the Niger Delta affects water and, therefore, the health of the environment and the people. Eke's work with water and acid rain continued in a version of this work called *Water Drop* in 2008, which had sachets of acid rain suspended in the shape of a large water drop or toxic cloud. Eke's has exhibited different iterations of this piece internationally.

Inspiration for this piece, as well as the next iteration, *Shields,* comes from Eke's personal experience in Port Harcourt, Rivers State, in the Niger Delta. The lack of governmental controls on pollution or mandating safe environmental practices for oil companies operating in the area ostensibly gives them license to pollute without consequence. His firsthand experience of the health effects of oil extraction pollution inspired several pieces of work:

> I was working outside in the rain. In two days, I discovered skin irritation from toxic chemicals that go into the atmosphere from the industries. The emissions from the industries come down when it rains. I was not surprised, as Port Harcourt has a lot of industries, especially in the manufacturing and the oil production. Then I came to think about not just myself but the people who live around the area. What about the aquatic life? What about the vegetation? (Eke in Weintraub 2012: 161).

The pollution from oil extraction and refinement touches every aspect of life. Tobenna Okwuosa, a Nigerian artist and art critic, writes about the significance of Eke's work for Nigeria. He begins with contextualising the ecological situation in the Niger Delta. 'The traditional food supply from agriculture and fishing is no longer feasible, made impossible by constant acid rain and the oil pouring out of the rusty or sabotaged pipelines; the fish are dying in the contaminated water' (Ursprung in Okwuosa 2013: 63). The oil extraction in the Niger Delta is 'dirtier' than in Global North countries that have stricter (and enforced) environmental protections (Nixon 2013), also making it harder for local people to access other sources of food and water or even alternative livelihoods. As River-based peoples across the Delta find their way of life and traditions decimated, Shell and others continue to extract oil, violently squashing oppositional movements with the help of the Nigerian government.

People in Nigeria are forced to buy drinking water because of the lack of access to potable water supplies. It is more expensive than in many Global North countries. Drinking water is packaged in plastic sachets that are made of petroleum and labelled 'pure water' although this is often not the case. Contaminated water is often consumed by necessity in Nigeria because of the lack of reliable water infrastructure and the prohibitive cost for many. The plastic water sachets are single-use and are prevalent as litter, further contaminating the environment (Okwuosa 2013).

Eke was interested in the materiality of water and making work to highlight the devastating effects of its pollution:

> Water is a precious natural medium/resource with universal language. It occupies the largest part of the earth, but has been disrespected, polluted, and contaminated with the advent of industrialization ... I am interested in exploring water in ways that can examine global, human and environmental issues. (Eke 2008 in Okwuosa 2013: 66)

Eke takes water as his subject in several of his pieces, expanding and reimaging *Acid Rain* in different forms. The acid rain and contaminated water of the Niger Delta have global connections to everyday oil usage and the Shellmex sign in MERL and the London-based banks that fund the operations in *Oil City*. He draws out these invisible connections through striking installations on the materiality of polluted water.

Eke's work *Shields* (2005 – 2007) is an installation made of thousands of discarded water sachets gathered from litter on the streets. It features the soiled sachets, in the state they were found, sewn into transparent raincoats and umbrellas. These are the shields of the title – rain gear to protect against acid rain. For Okwuosa, the work 'problematise[s] the apocalyptic consequences of

Figure 1 Image of Shields, 2005-2007 © Bright Ugochukwu Eke. (Courtesy Axis Gallery, New York)

air and water pollution which is made worst by the littering of these non-biodegradable materials in our seriously corroded environments' (Okwuosa 2013: 67). The work features 120 coats and 60 umbrellas. It has been exhibited in gallery spaces with the raincoats suspended from above, giving off a ghostly and haunted air.

The work has been shown in Senegal, Nigeria, Germany, Algiers and Greece. In Lagos, community members donned the rain gear and paraded through the streets in a performance that Eke described as 'a public demonstration of the blighted state of the source of life on Earth' (in Weintraub 2012: 163). The performance that animates the 'shields' creates another dimension. A photo of the work (see Figure 1) features six presumably Nigerian men standing in a grassy field, looking directly into the camera, wearing full-length raincoats made of sewn-together soiled water sachets. Three of them are holding umbrellas made in the same way, while the other three men have the hoods up to protect themselves from the rain. The image is one of defiance as the men stand in solidarity against the harmful environmental pollutants and all the corrupt colonial and capitalist systems that facilitate them. There is an apocalyptic sense as well, using garbage to create necessary protections. Apocalyptic imagery is something that the Niger Delta is associated with after being ravaged by oil and gas extraction. As Okwuosa has proclaimed, the 'Niger Delta area is one of the most ecologically disturbed and endangered spaces in the world' (2013: 66). The performance of *Shields* embodies this, making visible the connection between ecologically damaged spaces and the marginalised bodies that are subjected to that damage.

Shell has been extracting oil from the Niger Delta since the 1950s, with seemingly little regard for the ecological and social consequences of their operations. After several oil spills, sabotage, and lawsuits, Shell is now trying to exit their onshore Niger Delta operations to focus on the 'less problematic' offshore extraction (Osuoka 2024). At the time of writing, the sale is being protested against by local people of the Niger Delta as they feel that Shell is trying to evade responsibility and accountability for the damage caused. The sale would mean that Shell has no incentive to remediate the area and compensate the people for the environmental and human rights abuses they have caused (Osuoka 2024). I have written elsewhere about performances that engage with the devastating consequences of oil extraction in the Niger Delta, including the gender-based violence depicted in the play *Then She Said It* (2002) by Osonye Tess Onwueme (Woynarski 2020a), as well as work that references the untimely killings of Ken Sara-Wiwa and eight other Ogoni activists, such as *Atmospheric Forces* (2021 -) by Sue Palmer and Sheila Ghelani (Woynarski 2025). Eke's work joins a history of activist artwork coming out of the Niger Delta. Okwuosa characterises this work under the genre of Niger Delta Visuals, a companion to Niger Delta Literature (2013). These have been powerful tools in capturing the world's attention towards the environmental injustice being suffered in the Niger Delta. Renowned (and wrongfully executed) Ogoni activist Ken Sara-Wiwa wrote: 'the most important thing for me is that I've used my talents as a writer to enable the Ogoni people to confront their tormentors. I was not able to do it as a politician or a businessman. My writing did it' (quoted in Nixon 2013: 105). The artistic work about oil extraction has captured the global imagination and helped to partially hold oil companies accountable.[8]

Rob Nixon describes Nigeria as resource-cursed, which means 'the greater a state's reliance on a single mineral resource, the greater the chances that state is undemocratic, militaristic, corruption riddled, and governed without transparency or accountability' (2013: 69). Nigeria is essentially the poster child for corruption because of the resource curse. The oil and gas Nigeria produces

---

[8] The untimely execution of Ken Sara-Wiwa and his fellow Ogoni 9 activists by the Nigerian government sparked global outrage. His son brought a lawsuit against Shell for human rights abuses, which Shell settled out of court, agreeing to pay $15.5 million into a trust for the Ogoni people. Shell also moved their operations out of Ogoniland, relocating to other parts of the Niger Delta, without cleaning up the damage it inflicted. Nixon writes that the World Wildlife Fund estimates it would cost upwards of $6 billion for environmental reparation of the area (Nixon 2013: 125).

(96 per cent of its export revenue and 80 per cent of government income) makes a small number of the political class, corporations and corporate workers extremely wealthy while most of the country lives on less than a dollar a day (Nixon 2013; Platform 2005). In fact, oil has made most of the population worse off, despite the exorbitant sums of money flowing into the country from oil extraction. The Niger Delta is also under threat due to the climate crisis and rapid sea level rise, which are all exacerbated by oil and gas extraction.

The Niger Delta is the size of England and home to over 40 different ethnic groups or 'micro-minorities' (Nixon 2013), including Sara-Wiwa's Ogoni. These micro-minorities were promised economic justice after Nigerian independence in 1960, with the government promising to return 50 per cent of the revenue derived from extraction practices. However, despite this constitutional promise, the Delta peoples have received less than 1.5 per cent (even less in practice). This is because 'the Ogoni lack the political leverage and constitutional protections to lay claim to the wealth that has been stripped from their land' (Nixon 2013: 106). Nigerian borders are the ones drawn by British colonialism in the early 1900s, encompassing more than 300 ethnic groups. The continuing legacy of colonialist borders leaves the micro-minorities without political capital and with devastated land, water and livelihoods.

The ecological connections between London and the Niger Delta continued as the first crude oil out of the Delta went to London:

> Two hundred ton barges shuttled the oil to two storage tanks in Port Harcourt; from there it was then shipped to the Shellhaven refinery at the mouth of the River Thames. Within a few weeks of its arrival, Nigerian gasoline was fuelling automobiles in and around London, the new symbols of post-war British prosperity. (Watts 2008: 36)

Shell is responsible for the environmental injustices in the Niger Delta used to fuel London's prosperity. The other connection, rarely discussed according to Platform, is 'the role of London-based banks – who participate in Nigerian corruption by facilitating transfers and profiting in the process' (Platform 2005). *The Next Gulf* (Rowell et al. 2005) is a book associated with Platform's memorial to Ken Sara-Wiwa. It includes a map of 'The Niger Delta in London' which details the institutions and companies in London related to Shell's oil operations in Nigeria. Massey writes about the map: 'if all the sources and links in the oil commodity chain and its multifarious supports were mapped, the centre of London would be crowded with references . . . part of their aim is to look beyond the local place, to trace its implications around the world' (2011: 205). The influence of London on the lives of those living in the Niger Delta is made visible through the overlay of places on the map. These bio-urban ecological relationships are revealed as 'the ordinary invisibility' of 'chains of quotidian connection' (2011: 205). The political and financial decisions of London, as well as the everyday consumer practices, are directly related to Shell digging, mining and extracting oil from the Niger Delta.

Both *Acid Rain* and *Shields* draw a clear line from oil extraction in Nigeria to its effects on the bodies of those who live there. Stacey Alaimo writes about the human/environment interconnection: 'potent ethical and political possibilities emerge from the literal contact zone between human corporeality and more-than-human nature ... [which] underlines the extent to which the substance of the human is ultimately inseparable from "the environment"' (Alaimo 2010: 2). Eke's work sits in this contact zone and explores the possibilities that emerge from it. The iteration of *Shields* that features humans activating the piece through performance, donning the raincoats, draws the focus to the bodies and the substance of what is human. There is a vulnerability to these male bodies under the transparent, stitched-together raincoats. The materiality of oil is so potent that it transforms the air, soil and water, which then affects bodies through acid rain and lack of crops and aquatic life. The flimsy, old plastic sachets used to make the raincoats gesture to the fragility of the 'shield' in effectively protecting the wearer from the environmental toxins. The materiality of oil is also enacted through the political and social contexts that maintain its dominance. Eke's work calls for further interrogation of the ethical and political choices made (usually in global cities like London and Washington) that support the fossil fuel-intensive practices and create this unequal exposure.

Eke's work gestures to a way in which oil can transform environments and bodies. In a history of oil cultures, Frederick Buell describes the proliferation of oil-based products post World War II. The chemistry that produced wartime weapons was applied to everyday items, turning oil into new products, 'from plastics to pharmaceuticals, printer inks to pesticides. It changed into what people dressed in, evacuated into, viewed, and even ate ... Oil thus now reappeared as an agent of chemical *and* social metamorphosis' (Buell 2012: 290). Oil's materiality continues to transform, from fossil to fuel, to plastic and pollution. Eke's work extrapolates this negative metamorphosis of drinking water being polluted. This leads people to have to purchase water in bags, shaping the environment of plastic debris, while the bodies of Niger Delta residents are being transformed by acid rain.

Eke's work makes visible the materiality of bio-urban relationships. They are living relationships that affect bodies, demonstrating that humans are part of the more-than-human world, even in urban centres. Humans are thus interconnected with the environment and susceptible to all of the uneven effects that entail, with marginalised and racialised humans often bearing the brunt of the burden in this relationship. The materiality of oil, as well as the political and capitalist decisions, radiate out from global metropolises. The oil-dependency of global cities and financial centres such as London impacts the human and more-than-human bodies of Nigeria. Eke's work exposes the costs of this dependency.

Can I Live?

From London to Port Harcourt to the experience of a Nigerian diaspora climate activist in London, these cities and bodies are all connected through oil extraction and global oil commodity chains. The final performance of this section centres on the experience of a London-based man of Nigerian heritage who takes a decolonising approach to climate activism, highlighting his lived experience of the global ecologies and the accelerating climate crisis.

2021: It is a year into the pandemic, and I am excited to watch the digital tour of a new performance by the renowned theatre company Complicité. I open my laptop and click the link at the designated time. The prerecorded piece starts with writer and performer Fehinti Balogun in a small flat framed through a Zoom screen, telling us about moving back in with his mother during lockdown. Just as I worried about having to sit through another Zoom performance, the walls of the flat come down in a dramatic fashion, and the camera moves out to a wide angle. We are on the stage of the Barbican Theatre in London, and there is a live band scoring Balogun's narrative. Throughout the next 60 minutes, Balogun speaks directly to the audience, describing the details of global temperature rises with animations and digital effects. At other times, he tells personal stories, interspersed with lively and emotional hip-hop songs and spoken word poetry. Balogun details his autobiographical journey into the climate activist movement and its whiteness. He speaks about his Nigerian heritage and the ecological devastation happening in Nigeria. He powerfully links the history and ongoing legacies of colonialism to the current climate crisis.

Balogun centres his experience in the climate movement as a Black British-Nigerian man. He wonders why he is often the only person of colour in a room at activist events: 'Why don't any of these people look like me? Most of the people at these protests were white and middle class. And it seemed like it's been like that for the last 30 years. Do people like me not know? Do we not care?' (Balogun 2021). He seeks to understand the whiteness of the climate movement when the effects of climate breakdown are being disproportionately felt by those most marginalised in places like Africa. Balogun details the multiple and complex forces that many African and African diaspora people face that can

Figure 2 Image from Can I Live? by Fehinti Balogun, 2021.
(Photo by David Hewitt)

make participating in the climate movement difficult and even too risky. He spoke to friends and family to try to understand the perceived lack of care and unwillingness to act. He discovered that many people in his circle are busy trying to survive and therefore do not have the time or resources to do things like protest. Balogun talks about how much riskier it is for him as a Black man to have a confrontation with police at protests. He says there is a privilege to joining the climate movement because the climate crisis is a class crisis as well. It takes time and resources to participate, which are privileges that cannot be enjoyed if you don't have time to think about anything else other than surviving. He talks about how this activism contravenes his family's three principles of 'Keep your head down. Do your work. Don't get into trouble'. By infusing his personal stories and emotional vulnerability with climate change data, animations and lively hip-hop and rap (see Figure 2), his identity and cultural experience are foregrounded both aesthetically and narratively. In so doing, the dominant white aesthetic of climate art (which follows the whiteness of the climate movement) is displaced.

Can I Live? Features a memorable statistic that 'A 1.5 degree increase [in average temperature] would mean drought in West Africa for 6 months' and would hit North Africa harder (Balogun 2021). Balogun says, 'climate change is modern colonialism' (2021). It is what Balogun describes as 'climate genocide' (2021). He references the slave plantations in the Caribbean that facilitated the growth and profits of the British Empire. He identifies the Industrial Revolution as the beginning of our dependence on fossil fuels and the rise of CO2 emissions. There is an animation of him holding the earth, rapping about how more emissions, the hotter it gets. He performs the following:

> Slavery plantations in the Caribbean provided the raw material for industrial change and growth in the British Empire.
> But it goes deeper.
> Fused with that history of slavery
> are the genocides and the conquests the liberation of oil by liberators
> that deliberate the price of liberation whilst polluting all the soil
> Shout out to Shell
> the moment when our relationship with living things became one-sided and disharmonious.
> We profit, forget and move on.
> We profit, forget and move on (Balogun 2021)

Here, Balogun is referring to the Anthropocene (the geological age of the human) and the influence of colonialism on the current climate crisis as 'the moment when our relationship with living things became one-sided' (2021). As scholars Adams and Mulligan note colonialism 'transformed nature, creating new landscapes, new ecologies and new relations between humans and non-human nature; in the process, it created new ideologies of those relationships' (2003: 1). These are ideologies of violent extraction and exploitation, based on sacrificing certain (often racialised) humans and more-than-humans for the sake of profitability. However, as Kathryn Yusoff (2018) has pointed out, it is important to counter the homogenising and universalising narrative of the Anthropocene that all humans are equally responsible.[9] Just as the impacts of the climate crisis are asymmetrical and uneven, so is the responsibility. Colonialist 'powers' spread an ideology of domination and extraction across the globe, which is still being felt today. Scholars Szeman and Boyer write that 'only certain populations of the world drove the globalization of fuel-intensive life, and they did so through centuries of colonizing violence. More than that, northern white masculinity continues to epitomize the apex species logic of entitlement that has brought us to our current situation' (2017: 9). Balogun draws out these distinctions and nuances, countering the universalising 'northern white masculinity' through his personal experiences of being a Londoner from the Nigerian diaspora.

---

[9] I have written previously about countering the idea of the Anthropocene through Indigenous performance (Woynarski 2020a).

The Shellmex sign continues to resonate as Balogun raps 'Shout out to Shell', and the extractivist violence of their oil operations in the Niger Delta, as the 'liberators' of the oil, pollute the soil. The Niger Delta formed one of the three corners of the Atlantic Triangle of enslavement, where the barter purchases of enslaved people happened. Enslaved people were then forcefully transported to the Americas to work on plantations producing tobacco and sugar, which was then shipped to Britain and Europe. Platform details the London connection, 'London was pivotal in this triangle, profiting from the slave trade and coordinating the export of guns and other items to the Delta as goods to facilitate barter' (Platform 2005). After decades of British colonialism, oil is now recreating this triangle, with the majority of what is produced in Nigeria travelling across the Atlantic. 'Once again resources pour out of the Delta and guns flow in – though this time London shares it role with Washington' (Platform 2005). Colonialism continues to remake itself in different formations, this time using oil.

Balogun's performance features a catchy song, 'Why Don't We Talk About It', about how little his Nigerian family talk about the devastating and deadly consequences of the climate crisis and the attendant politics of oil extraction.

> Why don't we talk about the pollution and poisoning of rivers and streams caused by Shell. or the British colonial assault on Nigerian oil since 1905. Why don't we talk about the blood-stained brotherhood of colonisation and oil. How can just less than half of the population live in extreme poverty when NIGERIA is the biggest oil exporter in Africa?' (2021).

In the song, he wonders why his aunties and uncles don't talk about the major flooding, the deforestation and desertification, the polluted waterways, and the natural gas flaring, instead of telling him about the modern urban developments of Lagos (such as state-of-the-art stadiums and shopping centres). He concludes that 'we can only look at the positive capitalist structures because if we saw what's really happening, we might see how little we've progressed. How much colonisation still exists' (Balogun 2021). This is a reassertion of what Katherine McKittrick calls plantation logics, or the idea that 'the plantations of transatlantic slavery underpinned a global economy' driving wealth into the metropolitan centres while exploiting and marginalising the racialised 'other', enforced through violence (McKittrick 2013: 3). These plantation logics have structured the colonialist economic 'othering' that renders some racialised humans and more-than-humans sacrifices for fuel-intensive lifestyles.

Throughout the performance, Balogun's anger, frustration, confusion, sadness and tears are potently present. The mix of his personal stories and emotional responses with the geopolitics of the climate crisis, his sense of helplessness and climate anxiety, allows the audience to interrogate the complexities of this modern colonialism. The ending includes 20 or so different activists of colour, seated in the audience of the Barbican, each taking a turn to stand up and describe the activist and community-organising work they are doing across the UK. In a reversal of Balogun being the only person of colour in the room, there is a strong sense of community building and solidarity, which gives Balogun hope. It is a powerful moment to end on. In this rare instance of a decolonial portrayal of the climate crisis on the British stage, the performance ends with an upbeat song that captures this sense of unlikely hope.

The performances in this section follow the lines of engagement with oil through urban ecologies: from the financing and profiting from oil in London to the local effects of extraction in the Niger Delta. The works make visible our 'energy unconscious' (Szeman and Boyer 2017: 9) or the way in which our fossil fuel dependencies (particularly in the Global North) are rendered invisible in order to preserve the status quo and protect the flow of profits to centres of power in global cities. To awaken the 'energy consciousness' is to be made aware of the material effects of oil extraction on humans and more-than-humans. For Szeman and Boyer, this means 'to shed light on the fuel apparatus of modernity, which is all too often invisible or subterranean, but which pumps and seeps into the groundwaters of politics, culture, institutions, and knowledge in unexpected ways.' (2017: 9). The saturation of oil across structures, politics, health and environmental justice is deeply rooted in ideologies of colonialism. *Oil City, Acid Rain, Shields* and *Can I Live?* each reveal an aspect of this saturation in modern urban life. Arising from London, as a world city, the revelations in the performances connect to local life in Port Hardcourt, Nigeria and Alberta, Canada. They extend the bio-urban towards an understanding of far-reaching material consequences reverberating from global cities through tracing the commodity of oil.

3 Urban Futures against the Apocalypse

Pervasive future ecological visions of cities are often built on representations of apocalypse, with natural disasters destroying urban environments. Unfortunately, these visions are not happening in the future but are an immediate reality for many. In 2024 alone, there were deadly heatwaves, droughts, floods, wildfires and hurricanes across the globe, devastating ecosystems, habitats, homes, food supplies and livelihoods.

These representations of apocalypse, according to geographer Erik Swyngedouw, foreclose the possibilities of other socioenvironmental imaginaries (2007: 13–14). In this section, I look at performances that ask: what happens if we reject the apocalyptic futures of the city? What happens if we envision futures not based on devastation and destruction? How can we live together in more just and ecological ways? Rather than representations of the end of the world, this section focuses on performances that imagine the urban futures in hopeful and pluralistic ways based on community action. The performances in this section represent different visions of futures based on regeneration and equality from different places: somewhere unspecified in Canada (*The Unplugging*), places across the UK (*The Strategy Room*) and urban green spaces in Mexico City (*Proyecto TEJIDOS*). Together, they make a case for rejecting the idea of apocalypse in favour of radical ideas for hopeful futures.

The performances resonate with the 2023 theme of Climate Change Theatre Action (CCTA), which was 'All Good Things Must Begin', inspired by Octavia Butler's work.[10] It is about the idea that climate crisis requires an imaginative leap, as the CCTA website states:

> we will create a just and regenerative world only if we dare to imagine it first, and use that vision to guide us through the difficulties. We all need to be solarpunks and envision radical pluralistic futures where nature and community thrive, and where we reject the apocalypse and embrace counterculture, post-capitalism, and decolonization. (CCTA 2023)

The performances included in this section all envision pluralistic futures and community thriving. They dare to make these imaginative leaps through envisioning a post-electricity world in which Indigenous values build community in *The Unplugging* (2014) by Yvette Nolan, through participatory policy engagement with community members in *The Strategy Room* (2023) by Fast Familiar and through reclaiming of urban green spaces for artistic community interventions in *Proyecto TEJIDOS* (2018–2022) by ecoscenographer Aris Pretelin-Esteves.

Amitav Ghosh famously wrote that 'the climate crisis is also a crisis of culture, and thus of imagination' (2017: 9). Like Octavia Butler, we need to imagine the futures we want to see in order to take steps towards realising them. This is the role of theatre and performance: embodied artistic encounters that spark imagination, and envision new forms of coexistence in decolonising, just and hopeful ways. While it is unlikely that the effects of the climate crisis can or will be fully reversed, the futures imagined by the performances here accept the situation but look for ways of moving forward together. The three performances below are brought together because they each do this in unique ways, extending the bio-urban through a focus on community.

---

[10] Butler, O. (2000) 'A Few Rules for Predicting the Future', *Essence Magazine*, May, pp. 165–166.

The Unplugging

The Unplugging (2014), by renowned Algonquin playwright and director Yvette Nolan, imagines a near future in which there has been a worldwide power cut. The world is suddenly left without power and the Internet. The play opens with two women trudging across a snowy landscape, one dragging a toboggan full of supplies. They have recently been kicked out of their community for being too old to be of use (i.e. not of childbearing age). They are searching for shelter, a cabin one of them remembers from a time before. They find the cabin and must rely on traditional Indigenous knowledge for survival in a harsh Canadian winter. As they begin to thrive, a young man named Seamus arrives from the community that exiled them to infiltrate their lives, steal their supplies and extract their survival knowledge. The women must decide if they should let him in, teach him, and help the community that rejected them. It premiered at the Arts Club Theatre in Vancouver in 2012, followed by a run at Factory Theatre in Toronto in 2015.

Based on an Athabaskan story, *Two Old Women* (told by Velma Wallis), which is set in pre-contact time, Nolan's story of two women (Elena and Bern) is adapted to the near future. They are two Indigenous women in their 50s. Once they are on their own, they learn to work together, access their traditional knowledge and develop survival skills. Bern is from Winnipeg and Elena is from Saskatoon. Like many Indigenous people, they lived in the city and not in remote parts of the land before the power cut. They drew on knowledge from spending time with their grandparents and elders. Elena had knowledge of the land, plants, hunting, seasonal food growing, preservation and cooking, which she learned from her grandmother, and although she has not used it for some time, she is able to share it with Bern.

Bern and Elena's experience of Indigenous urban migration is typical for many Indigenous peoples in North America. Heather Dorries (Sagkeeng First Nation) contends that colonialism has defined Indigeneity and urbanity and they 'have often been understood as antithetical terms and defined in opposition' (2023: 110), particularly in the context of Canadian settler colonialism. Despite many Indigenous people living in cities, Dorries argues that cities are not thought of as Indigenous spaces and therefore serve the colonial project of Indigenous assimilation/erasure. 'The assumption that cities are not Indigenous spaces is reflected in urban policies that not only ignore Indigenous history and territoriality but also further entrench colonial displacement and dispossession through processes of gentrification, policing and surveillance, and other forms of structural racism' (112). Indian reserves in Canada were designated away from cities and as temporary until assimilation (into cities) or 'die outs' happened. Therefore, policymakers were puzzled by the large number of Indigenous peoples migrating to cities and devised the term 'urban Indian' in the 1960s to account for people who lived 'off reserve' in centres of industrial and economic opportunity. Dorries argues for recognising how Indigeneity and urbanity are co-produced rather than Indigeneity as a fixed identity category and the urban as a static spatial container. While Bern and Elena find survival in a remote setting, the play does not set up a binary between nature and urban. For Dorries, Indigenous urbanism is 'a set of practices that connect people to place by highlighting practices of relationality and life making' (116). In *The Unplugging*, because of the power cut, there is a lack of differentiation between the city and more rural or remote places. Life and place-making happen in this world through a set of practices that embody Indigenous values for Bern and Elena, in opposition to the settler-based community that exiled them for not being 'useful'.

In some ways, the world of *The Unplugging* can be seen as post-apocalyptic. The unplugged world is littered with dead things as Elena tells Bern, 'Hatchets and knives and guns and tons of useless dead things. Dead cars, dead stereos, dead computers, dead telephones, dead rockets, dead, dead, dead' (Nolan 2013: 7). Food is scarce as canned goods are running out as winter approaches. Libraries have been looted for fuel, and people are getting sick. Nolan says she set the play in a post-apocalyptic ruin 'because of my own belief that human beings cannot or will not pull ourselves back from the brink of annihilation, I destroyed most of planet' (Nolan 2015: 89). However, within this destroyed world, there is a more hopeful message about Indigenous community values.

Daniel R Wildcat (Muscogee, Yuchi) has written about the climate crisis as another forced removal of Indigenous peoples, particularly in the Arctic and surrounding areas. After forced removals from their lands in the now United States on the Trail-of-Tears and residential boarding schools, climate change is now forcing yet another removal. For the Indigenous peoples who are directly affected by climate change, Wildcat feels a sense of anger and frustration for a crisis they did not create. 'The anger results from yet another removal scenario for Indigenous peoples who are facing catastrophic and deadly situations in which, strictly speaking, their Indigenous cultures had no part' (2009: 8). This frustration and anger are echoed in *The Unplugging* for Bern who exclaims 'This is how we got into this situation in the first place, people indiscriminately taking and using and wasting without any thought to the future' (Nolan 2013: 31). For Wildcat, 'hopefulness resides with those who are willing to imaginatively reconstitute lifeways emergent from the nature-culture nexus' (2009: 20). The nature-culture nexus (similar to the nature-urban nexus) is what Wildcat refers to as a 'symbiotic relationship' which recognises the interconnectedness of humans, the natural environmental and more-than-human 'relatives' we are dependent on. For him, the ability to imagine other ways of living, recognising this dependence, is where hopefulness lies. We see this in the play as Elena and Bern relearn the traditional practices of their ancestors of living off the land, in seasons. They make snares to catch rabbits for rabbit stew (*pebeepebonbon*), they shoot a moose and make jerky to preserve the meat through the winter, they plant things to grow in the next season, all marking time by the moon. Returning to this knowledge was not something they had to do before in their urban living experiences.

The Unplugging suggests that looking to traditional knowledge is needed to face the future. However, it avoids the romanticised tropes of Indigenous peoples being stuck in the past. Nolan depicts the two older women building a new life together based on Indigenous values: 'The core values of women, consensus, generosity, elder respect, and connection to land all formed the base of the world that Bern and Elena begin to build together' (Nolan 2015: 92). Echoing these values, Zoe Todd (Métis) writes about some of the Indigenous principles she has learnt from her Indigenous teachers needed to face climate-changed futures: 'reciprocity, love, accountability, and care are tools we require to face uncertain futures and the end of worlds as we know them' (2016: n.p.). Bern and Elena come to accept these teachings as well, understanding that these tools of care, love, reciprocity and accountability are the best chance for future living in peaceful and just ways. The rebuilding required in post-power landscapes like *The Unplugging* needs to turn away from the ideological values that created the situation (patriarchal capitalist colonialism), instead turning towards Indigenous principles.

When Seamus, the younger settler man, shows up from their former community, saying he too has been exiled, Bern offers to share skills and teachings with him, as she feels it would be wrong not to: 'I can teach you to catch rabbit. And I can show you willow, and how to find water, and what is edible even though it's Snow Crust Moon' (Nolan 2014: 55). Seamus learns from Bern and then disappears, stealing supplies and food from the two women. Seamus was formerly a bike messenger in a busy city, and he felt aimless in his old life with no real ambition or goals or sense of purpose. He returns to Bern and Elena's cabin on the next moon with a peace offering, a trout he caught himself. He admits he was sent from the community that exiled the women to raid their supplies. However, he did not expect their generosity. He felt compelled to learn the traditional skills and take them back to the community because so many people were ill. After the power-hungry community leader died, the community began to talk about new leadership, about elder leaders. This is when Seamus returns to find Bern and Elena and asks them to consider coming back: 'I realize you have no reason to trust us, to trust me. But maybe if we can just sit, and talk, about possible futures' (Nolan 2014: 66). The implication is that Bern and Elena can come back in a leadership position as elders, transferring the new way of life they have built to the community and embodying the core Indigenous values of women-centred leadership, elder respect and leading through consensus and generosity. There is another possible future for them outside of the settler-colonial structures and power relations that led to the unplugging.

Indigenous thinking has a different temporal relationship with the idea of apocalypse and the Anthropocene compared to its place in Western thought. Indigenous peoples have already been through an apocalypse following European contact and colonialism. In Turtle Island, or what is now also known as Canada, this started in 1610 and continued with cultural genocide and through residential schools and now to the Missing and Murdered Indigenous Women crisis. Potawatomi scholar Kyle P Whyte argues that conceptualising the Anthropocene as a yet-to-come apocalypse erases Indigenous people's experience and stories, 'who approach climate change having already been through transformations of their societies induced by colonial violence' (2018: 224). Whyte suggests alternative ways of addressing the Anthropocene: 'Instead of dread of an impending crisis, Indigenous approaches to climate change are motivated through dialogic narratives with descendants and ancestors' (2018: 224). Instead of a future crisis or apocalypse, Indigenous peoples understand the climate crisis as an already unfolding and ongoing disaster. Worst-case climate scenarios are not future events but something ancestors have already experienced through ongoing settler colonialism and the attendant cultural genocide.

Whyte reflects on the idea that Anishinaabe ancestors would view the position of Anishinaabe today as a dystopian future. They would experience settler colonialism in the Great Lakes with the lack of collective agency, being forcibly removed from homelands, their histories not taught in school and lower health and wealth markers than the wider population, as a dystopian story (2018: 228). 'But our ancestors and future generations are rooting for us to find those secret sources of agency that will allow us to empower protagonists that can help us survive the dystopia or post-apocalypse' (Whyte 2018: 231). The unplugging event mirrors that of settler colonialism in its apocalyptic nature. The characters are able to find sources of agency in Indigenous core values and traditional knowledge, which empowers them to survive and even lead.

Grace Dillon (Anishinaabe/European descent) introduced the concept of Indigenous Futurisms, drawing on Afrofuturisms, as a genre of science fiction that centres on Indigenous ideas, writers, beliefs, histories, presents and futures. I read *The Unplugging* as Indigenous Futurism because of the ways it imagines the pasts, presents and potential futures. Dillon writes that 'Native apocalyptic storytelling, then, shows the ruptures, the scars, and the trauma in its effort ultimately to provide healing and a return to *bimaadizwin* [balance]. This is the path to a sovereignty embedded in self-determination' (2012: 9). Bern and Elena are forced into self-determination by necessity when rejected from their previous community. They eventually embrace this sovereignty and create relations of their own making. Dillon also describes Indigenous futurism as narratives of *biskaabiiyang*, which is an Anishinaabemowin word meaning 'returning to ourselves/returning to the woods'. This involves understanding how one is personally impacted by colonisation, relinquishing the baggage of that and 'recovering ancestral traditions in order to adapt in our post-Native Apocalypse world' (10). *The Unplugging* can be seen as a story of *biskaabiiyang* because Bern and Elena literally return to the woods to build their own survival stories based on ancestral traditions. Indigenous Futurisms provide a creative corrective to the apocalypse experienced as a result of settler colonialism.

In *The Unplugging*, rebuilding after the apocalypse involves remaking community through Indigenous principles. Transferring the urban experience of Indigenous peoples into a post-apocalyptic world, the characters imagine new ways of living together based on Indigenous core values. *The Unplugging* takes the imaginative leap to show us what Indigenous ancestors have already been through and survived, and how that traditional knowledge can be recuperated.

The Strategy Room

Moving to the UK in 2023, I examine how imaginative futures intersect with practical policy in participatory performance.

2023. I am seated around a rectangular table in a black box theatre at the University of Reading (UK) amongst an audience of university colleagues and students. I am excited to experience the new participatory work from Fast Familiar. There is an iPad in front of each of us. Our performance is facilitated by Rachel Briscoe of Fast Familiar. In an opening animation, we hear:

> 80 per cent of people in the UK are concerned about climate change. We know it's a big problem, but on our own, it's hard to know what to do about it, especially when there are so many other things to worry about. Right now, the UK isn't on track to meet its targets on climate change. That's bad news for everyone. We need a new plan ... So, you're here today to decide on a strategy for how to get there. (Fast Familiar 2023)

Over the next 90 minutes, we are tasked with deliberating over policies to help cities reduce their carbon emissions. We covered Food and Transport strategies. We watched introductory animations contextualising the problems in Food and

Transport before considering some of the proposed interventions. We heard 'postcards from the future', which are performers on video from a not-too-distant 'future' reporting back on how the policies are working in practice including the challenges and advantages to each. Throughout, we rated and then voted on the strategies based on what we would recommend for our local area.

The Strategy Room uses interactive performance methods to create an engaging, democratic and pleasurable experience for participants. Fast Familiar (led by Rachel Briscoe, Dan Barnard and Joe McAlister) is a group of UK-based theatre makers and artists from different creative and academic backgrounds who design 'audience-centric' experiences often using digital technology. Their work is usually interactive and participatory, driven by the audience and democratic principles of discussion, rating and voting, often using iPads.

The Strategy Room was commissioned by the Centre for Collective Intelligence Design (CCID) at Nesta (National Endowment of Science, Technology and Art) as a public engagement project on net zero policies. Part of their mission is to 'create a sustainable future where the economy works for both people and the planet' (Nesta 2023). They describe *The Strategy Room* as 'an immersive experience that combines facilitated deliberation, interactive polling and collective intelligence to identify the climate change policies that will best help local areas to reach net zero emissions' (Nesta 2023). However, Nesta's language of a sustainable future based on a net-zero economy is mired in a neoliberalist agenda. Brazilian Indigenous activist Ailton Krenak calls sustainability a myth: 'No company on this earth is sustainable, no matter what they say. But these companies and even whole sectors opportunistically appropriate the concept of sustainability for its marketing value' (Krenak 2020: 21). 'Net zero' may also hide carbon-intensive practices through a system of offsets, making zero carbon a spreadsheet trick. According to Fast Familiar, it is also not an inspiring concept that is easily understood by general audiences. They therefore made the choice not to use the language of 'net zero' in the performance itself.

Twelve local authorities in the UK took part in *The Strategy Room,* which reached over 640 participants. This ranged from places that were more urban to places that were more rural and those in between (mid-sized towns). The performance was facilitated for people who lived in the local area, as well as local authorities and councils (including elected officials) themselves. The piece contained three modules of the experience: Transport, Food and Domestic Heating, with each performance covering two of these. Each module had an introductory animation to give the climate change context for the issues. Fast Familiar assumed no prior knowledge of any of the participants. A series of recommendations was then generated through the

Performing Urban Ecologies

Figure 3 Image from Fast Familiar's The Strategy Room, 2023.

data analysis of all the experiences. These recommendations included which policies were popular and how to engage people through interactive means in climate policy discussions. They discovered that people viewed the policies in *The Strategy Room* much more favourably than when presented the same policies through a YouGov poll (Berditchevskaia et al. 2023: 24). This is likely because of the sense of agency the performance fostered, as well as an understanding of what the policies would look like in their everyday lives (through postcards from the future). The anonymised data generated from the performance (through the polls and voting) was then shared with the local governments.

The performances in the postcards from the future featured in the experience were the most innovative dramaturgical tool for allowing an audience to picture and understand what these policies would look like in practice and what their effect would be (see Figure 3). These testimonies were played at specific moments and provide further context to the discussions around the table. They were from three carefully selected characters that represented different geographies, viewpoints, identities and values. We followed the journey of a character from when the policy was announced to later seeing it in action and understanding the effect on their daily lives, including any challenges. The characters spoke about the policies in a personal way, detailing how they affected them and their social circles. These performances from the future helped the audience to envision and imagine what these policies could look like in their everyday lives in a not-too-distant future. In the performance I attended, we referred to them often, as well as trying to map them onto our local city context. Who did the policies work for? Who did they disadvantage? What might the unintended effects be? Would they work in our specific area?

Fast Familiar tested the performance experience extensively in draft form and recorded potential objections to the policies. Then, they incorporated responses into the show to generate further discussion.

One video postcard is from Stella, who lives in a big city in a not-too-distant future, describing how the public transportation subscription service worked in her area. She described a monthly subscription app that provides all of the options for travel – other than an individually-owned car. You input where you want to go and it gives you the quickest options based on traffic and weather, including electric buses, trains, the tube, e-scooters, e-bikes, different types of bikes like cargo bikes for putting your shopping in, e-mopeds, e-cars and hail-a-ride cars like Uber. There are also accessible travel options as well. She described the ease of the app for city living, allowing people to have an array of options at their fingertips with extra incentives for the lowest carbon options, like bikes. It allowed her to cycle more than she did when she had a bike collecting dust in her garden shed. She also talked about the disadvantages of the scheme, saying she didn't like to cycle in the rain, so had to take different options when that happened. Overall, Stella tells us that it was much easier and cheaper than private ownership of a car. Her testimony was then used to help us, as an audience, discuss, rate the policy and decide if we would recommend it in our area. The audience in my performance felt it was a good idea and could work well in Reading, UK.

The Strategy Room engaged with policies that are in circulation and under consideration in some cities, with a focus on what could reasonably be implemented by local governments in the near future and what could make a substantial difference in terms of carbon output. They chose policies at the level of system-change rather than individual change (such as individuals recycling more). The subscription transport options, called mobility-as-a-service, were modelled after examples such as the Jelbi app in Berlin (which features all of Berlin's public transport and mobility sharing services on demand in one app) and the BeeNetwork being rolled out in Manchester. Fast Familiar also worked closely with local authority partners in Lambeth, Sandwell and Southend-on-Sea, who were consulted on the kind of climate-friendly policies they were interested in and the kinds of challenges they expected. All the anonymised data from the performances was then sent to the local authorities so they could gauge what might be the best way to roll out some of the proposed policies. The local authority policymakers will be the ones deciding to implement different policies or not, but the responses from the audience gives them a rich picture of what community members find beneficial and why. The policies are from a restricted set of choices chosen by Fast Familiar, Nesta and the local authorities involved. It was telling that results showed that the policies that had clear community benefits were more popular than the ones with individual benefits, and community energy schemes were popular everywhere (Berditchevskaia et al. 2023: 4). Fairness and accessibility of each policy was a key factor in discussions, bearing out research that the UK public is concerned about these factors in net zero policies.

Rather than grieving for the future, the performance asks audiences the question: What if life could be better? Better for you, better for your community and better for the ecological environment? The town centre regeneration scheme was a popular policy in many of the performances. It involves creating a car-free area in the town centre, which is likely less convenient for many people, but it was popular because it also involved investment in beautification and shared use of the town centre, making it a more vibrant and nicer place to live. Countering the idea of the town centre as a solely commercial space, plans included nice places to walk and rest for leisure. The shared use scheme meant including non-commercial uses such as a café during the day, becoming an adult education centre in the evening. The mobility-as-a-service scheme was similar. It is less convenient than private car ownership, but it means there is no hassle trying to find parking, maintaining a car or bike, not to mention the cost of owning a car. It also benefits those who require on-demand accessible transport and those who find private car ownership cost-prohibitive. The benefits for people include improved air quality in their local cities, opportunities for exercise, accessible travel options, less traffic and potentially a reduction in traffic noise.

Hope and optimism for the potential to enact different ways of living marked the performance. Geographer Lesley Head notes: 'there is deep cultural pressure in the West not to be "a doom and gloom merchant". Hence, even when the evidence points towards the strong possibility of some catastrophic scenarios, the tendency is to focus on policy and action on the most optimistic end of the spectrum of possibilities' (Head 2016: 2). She separates hope from naïve optimism, instead looking to action to generate hope. Rather than doom and gloom, the audience of *The Strategy Room* left feeling hopeful: there are policies out there that could move the needle on climate and would improve our daily lives as well. All we need to do is enact them, which is, of course, much easier said than done. The policies are on the more optimistic end, but they are grounded in current realities of policies that are being enacted, trialled or considered. It is probably unlikely that all of these policies will be enacted as quickly as needed, and therefore they may not prevent catastrophic futures. However, they offer a way of envisioning a different way of living together as a first step. This is echoed by an audience member named June, an older woman participant from the performance in Sandwell: 'For me, it was just "the ice caps are melting" and "well, there is nothing we can do about it". But with you explaining the things that can slow it down, it is a positive insight into what the future would be like' (Fast Familiar 2023). It mobilises hope through the examples from the postcards from the future, understanding how everyday people's lives are being affected. It was also mobilised through the sense of action of voting and the opportunity to discuss the different policies with fellow audience members with different perspectives and experiences, who are also local community members.

In her blog detailing reflections from the project, Briscoe writes that 'we need more positive visions of the future. We really don't need any more dystopias or disaster scenarios – existing films, TV shows and books have those covered. We need to help people imagine what a positive future could be like, because, put simply, until we can imagine it, we can't make it happen' (Briscoe 2023). Fast Familiar drew on research from the UCL Climate Action Unit (led by Kris De Meyer) about the importance of action in climate storytelling. They believed that the public was ahead of policymakers in some ways, as they were more willing to embrace the net zero policies. They were interested in what narratives would convince policy makers to act (Barnard and Briscoe 2024). Researchers De Meyer et al. argue that 'climate change is primarily conceptualized as a threat we should be concerned about, rather than as something we know how to act on' (De Meyer et al. 2021: 1). This leads to a 'poverty of stories' because the existing narratives around climate change tend to focus on raising awareness and concern. Consequently, this then leads to a perceived 'lack of agency', or inability to act, among the general public. This creates a sense of only two limited options for action: consumer choices and climate activism. The authors argue that moving from issue-based stories to action-based stories would provide a sense of agency, as there is 'evidence from psychology and neuroscience showing that "in real life actions drive beliefs"—rather than awareness, beliefs or concern leading to behavior change' (De Meyer et al. 2021: 2). Drawing on these ideas, *The Strategy Room* offered action-based stories to the audience. The democratic approach to the performance felt empowering and gave us, as the audience, a sense of agency into future climate policies.

The Strategy Room offered a community-driven way of thinking about hopeful futures for cities in light of the climate crisis, understanding some of the complexities and intersections of urban ecologies. It further nuanced the bio-urban by taking into account all the different ways community members might have their lives affected by climate-friendly policies. It was forward-looking and focused on implementable ideas as a way of bypassing some of the debilitating inaction on climate.

In Mexico City, some of these ideas are being put in practice by reclaiming urban green spaces for community members through artistic intervention, as detailed below.

Proyecto TEJIDOS

A park in Mexico City. Colourful, woven fabric loosely knit together forms the dynamic costume of a performer (see Figure 4). Their skin is painted red, which complements the red, yellow and green brightly woven fabric draped around them. Their costume includes head-to-toe knits with fringe and a headpiece with beads and bells woven into it. The fringe is made from cut fabric pieces tied together. It is theatrical and eye-catching. The performer moves between large webs of knit material suspended from the trees as community members watch captivated. This is *Proyecto TEJIDOS* (2018–2022) from artist and ecoscenographer Aris Pretelin-Esteves.

TEJIDOS embodies practices of hope in climate changed urban contexts with local communities. Taking place in different urban green spaces in Mexico City, the artistic interventions of *TEJIDOS* were designed to be reparative of the current demarcated conditions of urban living. Urban green spaces (UGSs) can improve the quality of life for those who have access to them. Urban researchers in Mexico found that that ecologically, they 'sequester carbon, mitigate

Figure 4 Image from Pretelin-Esteves' TEJIDOS, 2019.
(Photo by Carlos Casasola)

air pollution, influence infiltration capacity, preserve biodiversity, and buffer temperature in cities' (Ayala-Azcarraga et al. 2023: 2). There are also social and community benefits as 'the presence of UGSs plays a fundamental role in establishing a support network by enhancing social cohesion within a community. This role facilitates interactions between diverse social groups associated with local economic improvement and strengthening local security' (Ayala-Azcarraga et al. 2023: 2). There are also individual psychological and mental health benefits to spending time in green spaces in cities as access 'promotes physical activity, mitigates stress levels, and contributes to mitigating mental exhaustion, depression' as well as improved cognitive and emotional health (Ayala-Azcarraga et al. 2023: 2). However, access to urban green spaces is uneven and a factor of environmental injustice. Mexico City is a large city (9.2 million people) with a prevalence of small urban green spaces in middle- to high-income neighbourhoods. The unequal distribution of urban green spaces means that the most marginalised people in the city have the least access to the urban green spaces and their attendant benefits (Ayala-Azcarraga et al. 2023: 2). Pretelin-Esteves' work with the *TEJIDOS* project aims to address some of this environmental injustice.

TEJIDOS consisted of three strands or actions. The first strand was community knitting workshops to generate the material used for the subsequent installations and performance costumes, called *Memorias Tejidos* (also called Urban Knitting), where memories and stories shared by community participants were knitted together. The second strand is *Tejedoras de Caminos* (also called Action Two: Performance), which contained performance elements using the materials generated in the first strand and involving performers and the public, weaving materials into the urban green spaces. The original concept was co-created with Pamela Eliecer. Realisation of the intricate costumes and headpieces by Estela Fagoaga and Miranda Aguayo.

The third strand was an audio-visual installation documenting the work and the stories shared (*Atlas de Memorias* or Installation). According to ecoscenographer Tanja Beer, the work 'literally weaves social and ecological components together in urban green spaces as a way of reconciling intercultural human-natural communities' (Beer 2021a: 113–114). The knitting workshops facilitated participatory engagement with memories of urban green spaces being reclaimed through traditional craft techniques. These were called woven memories, where anyone could come and learn to knit using recycled and discarded materials. Their creations would form the performance material and installation. The performance strand was a site-specific artistic response to the materials generated as well as the green spaces themselves. These were accompanied by scenic neighbourhood walks (also called Neighbourhood

Wanderers) that allowed community members to explore the sites in different ways, uncovering the hidden stories of the humans and more-than-humans that live there. These different strands of engagement created multiple modes of interaction and ways of noticing and reflecting at a slower pace, potentially disrupting the usual use of the space and fostering new social and ecological relationships.

The urban knitting workshops of Action One used discarded clothing and recycled fabrics, which were cut into strips to create 20,000 metres of recycled thread. The community participants then used hand weaving/knitting techniques to transform the recycled thread into mats, webs and pathways and installed them in urban green spaces as part of Action Two and Three. The knitting circles that were facilitated, both in the urban green spaces and online during the pandemic, created a space to share stories and memories of place. These included memories of the women using the park as a social space when their children were young, allowing them to make connections and form support networks. Pretelin-Esteves thinks of the hand knitting as a simple, repetitive act that relaxed the participants so they could 'listen and engage in dialogue with one another' (quoted in Beer 2021b). The project embodies Beer's ecoscenographic principle of co-creation, in its 'ability to make eco-creative processes and aesthetics visible and accessible, breaking down binaries between artists and the wider public' (Beer 2021a: 115). For Pretelin-Esteves, 'the fabric acts as a guiding axis for the project and is a metaphor for the multiple networks that connects us to the environment and the broader world' (quoted in Beer 2021b). It was also aimed at 'regenerat[ing] the social fabric and to resist the social-environmental crisis that we are experiencing right now in Mexico' (quoted in Beer 2021b). The designs reflected the histories and memories of the space, as well as imbuing care for its future. The fabric and knitting are both symbolic and material in the project. They call attention to the material waste produced by fast fashion, as well as its material intervention as artworks once they were installed in the urban green spaces.

Since 2018, the project has worked in urban green spaces around Mexico City, including Bosque de Chapultepec, Viveros de Coyoacan and Bosque de Aragón. One iteration of the project took place at the Jardín del Arte Sullivan (Sullivan Garden of Art) in Mexico City between 2019 and 2021. This was later presented at World Stage Design 2022 (Calgary, Canada) and Prague Quadrennial in 2019 (as a Pared Blanca project) and 2023. The Sullivan Garden of Art is an urban green space on the border between two neighbourhoods in Mexico City. This iteration involved a group of 30 women participants and, according to Pretelin-Esteves, the space was transformed from being 'no one's land' to a 'land for all beings' (Pretelin-Estéves 2023). This transformation resonates with some foundational theories of urban planning. For influential urban thinker Jane Jacobs, unpopular and/or underused city parks are troubling 'not only because of the waste and missed opportunities they imply, but also because of their frequent negative effects' (1992[1961]: 95). For an urban green space to be lively and vital, which are the qualities Jacobs uses to describe a successful park, it needs to have a mix of uses and activities: 'work, cultural, residential and commercial' (101). She writes that good design of city parks includes a centre 'stage setting' for people to spend time doing a mix of leisure and cultural activities: 'guitar players, singers, crowds of darting children, impromptu dancers, sunbathers, conversers, show-offs, photographers, tourists' (105). She writes that performance can transform urban green spaces, thereby increasing their liveliness. Fostering this liveliness was an important aspect of *TEJIDOS* and the impact it had on the urban green spaces of Mexico City. These temporary performances do not, however, shift the systemic barriers that might limit access to urban green spaces for certain people or inequalities around lack of time for leisure and culture or a sense of safety and accessibility in public spaces.

The project started with Pretelin-Esteves' idea of diverse participation: 'I started by reimagining the city as scenography, one in which we can all participate' (quoted in Beer 2021b). From this perspective, *TEJIDOS* was created to make connections to the local green spaces for different communities in Mexico City. The liveliness *TEJIDOS* created, bringing people into the green spaces to spend time, create memories, participate in cultural and artistic activities, fostered connections and engagement with the urban green spaces. She describes the encounters created by the project as being 'based on the flow of coexistence, to discover other ways of interacting and coping with the socio-political and environmental problems that affect the garden and its inhabitants' (Pretelin-Estéves 2023). In this way, the bio-urban lively relationships were made visible. Like *The Strategy Room*, the participatory knitting workshops generated ideas for urban spaces that could influence policy: 'These conversations and ideas are subsequently shared with institutions, committees, and neighbourhood associations to generate agreements and actions that will transform and take care of green spaces in the long term' (Pretelin-Esteves in Beer 2021b). The artistic interventions, through the three strands of the project, helped to transform the urban green spaces from 'no man's land' as Pretelin-Esteves articulates, to a space for all beings.

The goal was for the *TEJIDOS* interventions to create new ways of interacting together in the city. For Goh and Beer, the project 'demonstrates how embedding ecological and cultural narratives into site-specific activations reshapes our relationships with the places we inhabit' (2024: 314). The installations of recycled woven fabrics, with audio elements of memories, created spaces for the community to spend time, temporarily enlivening the urban green spaces and modelling a liveable future.

In theorising futures in performance, I draw on Lesley Head's concept of hope as an embodied practice, decoupled from the blind faith of optimism, full of conflicting yet generative emotions (2016: 11). She locates the practice within local, everyday spaces. These include things like community gardens, which 'have been much critiqued as too small, too local, too disconnected from the bigger more structural sources of economic power. But they are one space/time in which barely visible progressive futures might be rendered visible and imaginable' (2016: 77). We see this most explicitly in *TEJIDOS*, but all the performance works in this section imagine liveable futures through everyday spaces that might seem too small or too local at first glance. *The Unplugging, The Strategy Room* and *TEJIDOS*, practice hope by rendering different imagined futures of coexistence in more pleasureful or decolonised ways, rejecting future visions of apocalypse. Through performance-framed urban encounters, the works create a space for reframing the everyday and remaking our bio-urban relations in more hopeful and just ways.

Conclusion: Imagining a City

Two grand narratives of contemporary life—urbanisation and the climate crisis—not only intersect but fundamentally shape most aspects of how we live. Urbanisation has transformed the planet and redefined our relationship with it, often amplifying environmental and social inequalities. These inequalities manifest in diverse ways: limited access to urban green spaces, proximity to waste transfer centres, or the violence of extractive oil operations. Such eco-social disparities operate on both local and global scales. In the Global South, where urbanisation and industrialisation are accelerating, these injustices are even more pronounced, compounding the urgency of addressing these dual challenges of contemporary life.

The ten performances explored across these three sections provide a diverse sample of urban encounters that help us imagine, and occasionally enact, more vibrant, resilient, and equitable cities. I theorise how performing urban ecologies can reveal cities as living systems—deeply interconnected with 'nature' and shaped by environmental colonialism. These performances mobilise hope through decolonial, community-centred actions, offering a counterpoint to the exhausted narratives of dystopia. Urban eco-performances, such as *The Farm, Plum Tree Creek Project, The Strategy Room,* and *Proyecto TEJIDOS*, demonstrate tangible contributions to urban planning. These works influenced local government policies and community practices, fostering ways of living that respect and support the myriad bio-urban relationships essential to liveable, just cities.

If your city implemented all the ideas featured in the performances, life on this urban planet would be much better for humans and more-than-humans. Let's imagine that thriving farms would sit along highways, giving space for artists, children and animals, supporting the needs of diverse urban communities as in *The Farm*. Waste processing, including the labour needed to keep the cities clean and alive, would be made visible and fairly compensated – as in Ukeles' work with the New York City Sanitation Department. School children, elders, and community members would 'daylight' paved over waterways through cultural interventions, sharing meals together on site as in *Plum Tree Creek*. Indigenous presence would be foregrounded through Indigenous cultural practices at historical colonialist locations, acknowledging the role colonialism still plays in structuring cities, as in *Cultural Graffiti in London*. These performances reveal the different ways in which cities are alive and an entanglement of complex bio-urban relationships.

Let's stay in this imaginary city: the map of it includes how the global commodity of oil reaches out from the city to extraction sites like the Alberta Tar Sands and the Niger Delta. There is a transparency about how government, banks and oil companies work together to generate profit from environmentally disastrous projects, as in *Oil City*. In the city, there is an understanding of how local oil and petrol consumption impacts the micro-minorities of the Niger Delta, contaminating soil and groundwater and producing acid rain as in *Shields*. Climate crisis is understood as modern colonialism, following the same patterns as the exploitation as the transatlantic trade of enslaved peoples. Communities of colour organise in protest against these ongoing processes, as in *Can I Live?* The city understands and mitigates the global socio-ecological impact of its resource consumption with a strong sense of environmental justice.

Let's consider possible futures within this imaginary city: when faced with a power outage that halts modern ways of living, instead of reorganising in a patriarchal hierarchy, people turn towards Indigenous values of elder respect, reciprocity, women's leadership and care for one another as in *The Unplugging*. This decolonial approach to community living after the apocalypse is grounded in an understanding of the Indigenous apocalypse having already happened. Climate policy is considered and enacted through meaningful discussion with community members, who get a chance to consider how it would work for them and their neighbours, as in *The Strategy Room*. Urban green spaces are vibrant, mixed-use community sites that house multiple species as well as leisure and cultural events. They offer the community a chance to make artistic interventions, recuperating waste materials in the process, as in *Proyecto TEJIDOS*.

These works imagine multiple climate-changed futures that thrive through ecological, community-driven engagement.

Thinking beyond theatre and performance, theorising urban ecologies as ecodramaturgies offers ways to imagine and tell alternative stories. For urban studies, urban planning, geography and architecture, the work offered here provides models for communication, storytelling, affective responses and participatory practices. This allows for engagement with complexity, nuance, equality and community. While accepting the current ecological situation, the urban eco-performances featured here mobilise hope for new ways of relating and living together in cities.

References

Adams, W. M. and Mulligan, M. (2003) *Decolonizing Nature: Strategies for Conservation in a Post-colonial Era*. London: Earthscan.

Ahmadi, M. (2022) *Towards an Ecocritical Theatre: Playing the Anthropocene*. Abingdon: Routledge. https://doi.org/10.4324/9781003048749.

Alaimo, S. (2010) *Bodily Natures: Science, Environment, and the Material Self*. Bloomington: Indiana University Press.

Amin, A. and Lancione, M. (eds) (2022) *Grammars of the Urban Ground*. Durham: Duke University Press. https://doi.org/10.2307/j.ctv2x1npkj.

Amin, A. and Thrift, N. (2002) *Cities: Reimagining the Urban*. Cambridge: Polity.

Angelaki, V. (2019) *Theatre & Environment*. London: Red Globe Press.

Arons, W. and May, T. J. (eds) (2012) *Readings in Performance and Ecology*. New York: Palgrave Macmillan.

Ayala-Azcarraga, C., Diaz, D., Fernandez, T., Cordova-Tapia, F. and Zambrano, L. (2023) 'Uneven Distribution of Urban Green Spaces in Relation to Marginalization in Mexico City', *Sustainability*, 15(16), pp. 1–14, 12652. https://doi.org/10.3390/su151612652.

Balkan, S. and Nandi, S. (2021) 'Introduction: Reading Our Contemporary Petrosphere', in S. Balkan and S. Nandi (eds) *Oil Fictions: World Literature and Our Contemporary Petrosphere*. University Park, PA: Penn State University Press, pp. 1–18. https://doi.org/10.5325/jj.5233138.

Balogun, F. (2021) *Can I Live?* The Barbican, London [Digital Performance].

Bamboo Curtain Studios (2018) 'Art as Action for Ecology Movement: Case Studies of Bamboo Curtain Studio'. http://bambooculture.com/en/project-related/3463.

Bamboo Curtain Studios (2022) 'Art as Environment: A Cultural Action at the Plum Tree Creek'. http://bambooculture.com/en/project/2004.html.

Barnard, D. and Briscoe, R. (2024) 'Interview with Fast Familiar'. Interview by Lisa Woynarski.

Beer, T. (2021a) *Ecoscenography: An Introduction to Ecological Design for Performance*. Cham: Palgrave Macmillan.

Beer, T. (2021b) 'Encounter-Spaces and the City as Scenography: Interview with Aris Pretelin-Esteves (Mexico)', *Ecoscenography: Adventures in a New Paradigm for Performance Making*. https://ecoscenography.com/2021/02/03/encounter-spaces-and-the-city-as-scenography-interview-with-aris-pretelin-esteves-mexico/.

Bennett, J. (2010) *Vibrant Matter: A Political Ecology of Things*. Durham: Duke University Press.

Benton-Short, L. and Short, J. R. (2013) *Cities and Nature*. 2nd ed. New York: Routledge.

Berditchevskaia, A., Edgar, C. and Peach, K. (2023) *The Strategy Room: An Innovative Approach for Involving Communities in Shaping Local Net Zero Pathways*. London: Nesta.

Blight, S. (2018) 'Ogimaa Mikana'. www.susanblight.com/ogimaa-mikana.

Blissett, S. (2021) 'Algae Sympoiesis in Performance: Rendering-with Nonhuman Ecologies', *Performance Philosophy*, 6(2), pp. 117–136. https://doi.org/10.21476/PP.2021.62326.

Bo, Z. (2016) 'An Interview with Wu Mali', *Field: A Journal of Socially-Engaged Art Criticism*, Winter (3), pp. 151–164.

Brenner, N. (2013) 'Theses on Urbanization', *Public Culture*, 25(1), pp. 85–114. https://doi.org/10.1215/08992363-1890477.

Briscoe, R. (2023) 'The Strategy Room 1/3: Creating a Design Brief', 8 May. https://workroom.fastfamiliar.com/the-strategy-room-design-brief/.

Brown, V. (2020) 'To Be Black in the British Countryside Means Being an Outsider', *The Guardian*, 20 October. www.theguardian.com/commentisfree/2020/oct/20/black-woman-british-countryside-london-rural-village-stereotypes.

Buell, F. (2012) 'A Short History of Oil Cultures: Or, the Marriage of Catastrophe and Exuberance', *Journal of American Studies*, 46(2), pp. 273–293.

Carson, R. (2000) *Silent Spring*. London: Penguin.

Chaudhuri, U. (1995) *Staging Place: The Geography of Modern Drama*. Ann Arbor: University of Michigan Press.

Climate Change Theatre Action (2023) 'All Good Things Must Begin'. www.climatechangetheatreaction.com/ccta-2023/.

Coulthard, G. S. (2014) *Red Skin, White Masks: Rejecting the Colonial Politics of Recognition*. Minneapolis: University of Minnesota Press.

De Meyer, K., Coren, E., McCaffrey, M. and Slean, C. (2021) 'Transforming the Stories We Tell about Climate Change: From "Issue" to "Action"', *Environmental Research Letters*, 16(1), p. 015002. https://doi.org/10.1088/1748-9326/abcd5a.

Dillon, G. L. (2012) *Walking the Clouds: An Anthology of Indigenous Science Fiction*. Tucson: University of Arizona Press.

Dorries, H. (2023) 'Indigenous Urbanism as an Analytic: Towards Indigenous Urban Theory', *International Journal of Urban and Regional Research*, 47(1), pp. 110–118. https://doi.org/10.1111/1468-2427.13129.

Eckersall, P., Monaghan, P. and Beddie, M. (2014) 'Dramaturgy as Ecology: A Report from The Dramaturgies Project', in K. Trencsényi and B. Cochrane (eds) *New Dramaturgy*. London: Bloomsbury Methuen Drama, pp. 19–36. https://doi.org/10.5040/9781408177075?locatt=label:secondary_dramaOnline.

Eke, B. U. (2006) *Shields* [Installation and live performance].

Eke, B. U. (2008). Artist statement 2. http://u-bright.blogspot.com.br/search?updated-max=2009-10-31T16:03:00-07:00&max-results=7&start=7&by-date=false.

Ernstson, H. and Swyngedouw, E. (eds) (2019) *Urban Political Ecology in the Anthropo-obscene: Interruptions and Possibilities*. London: Routledge.

Evans, M. and Platform (2013) *Oil City* [Performance, ArtsAdmin Two Degrees Festival], London.

Fast Familiar (2023) 'The Strategy Room – documentation video'. https://youtu.be/i8llVDwRRfY?si=MsepjsXkwse7_vCv.

Finney, C. (2014) *Black Faces, White Spaces: Reimagining the Relationship of African Americans to the Great Outdoors*. Chapel Hill: The University of North Carolina Press.

Friedan, B. (1963) *The Feminine Mystique*. London: Victor Gollancz.

Galpin, P.-F. (2013) 'Cultivating the Human & Ecological Garden: A Conversation with Bonnie Ora Sherk'. http://curatorsintl.org/posts/cultivating-the-human-ecological-garden-a-conversation-with-bonnie-ora-sher.

Ghosh, A. (2017) *The Great Derangement: Climate Change and the Unthinkable*. Chicago: The University of Chicago press.

Gilbert, H. and Phillipson, J. D. (2015) 'Cultural Graffiti in London: Singing Life into Exhibitions and Embodying the Digital Document', *UNESCO Observatory Multi-Disciplinary Journal in the Arts*, 5(1), pp. 1–36.

Girardet, H. (2008) *Cities, People, Planet: Urban Development and Climate Change*. 2nd ed. Chichester: Wiley.

Goh, A. and Beer, T. (2024) 'Ecoscenographic Placemaking: A Cultural Approach to Creating Eco-sensitive Site-specific Work', *Theatre and Performance Design*, 10(4), pp. 300–320.

Goto, R., Shiu, M. and Mali, W. (2014) 'Ecofeminism: Art as Environment – a Cultural Action at Plum Tree Creek | Wead', 3 December. http://bambooculture.com/en/news/1743.

Grant, J., Pembina Institute for Appropriate Development, and Pembina Foundation (2013) *Beneath the Surface a Review of Key Facts in the Oilsands Debate*. Drayton Valley: The Pembina Institute.

Harvey, D. (1989) *The Condition of Postmodernity: An Enquiry into the Origins of Cultural Change*. London: Blackwell.

Harvey, D. (1993) 'The Nature of Environment: Dialectics of Social and Environmental Change', in R. Miliband and L. Panitch (eds) *Real Problems, False Solutions*. London: Merlin Press, pp. 1–51.

Head, L. (2016) *Hope and Grief in the Anthropocene: Re-conceptualising Human-Nature Relations*. London: Routledge. https://doi.org/10.4324/9781315739335.

Heynen, N., Kaika, M. and Swyngedouw, E. (eds) (2006) *In the Nature of Cities: Urban Political Ecology and the Politics of Urban Metabolism*. London: Routledge.

Hough, M. (2004) *Cities and Natural Process: A Basis for Sustainability*. 2nd ed. London: Routledge.

Huarcaya, S. and Phillipson, J. D. (2013) 'The Artist Sings: Peter Morin in Conversation'. https://vimeo.com/119944337.

Jacobs, J. (1992 [1961]) *The Death and Life of Great American Cities*. London: Vintage.

Klein, N. (2007) 'Baghdad Burns, Calgary Booms', *The Nation*, 31 May. www.thenation.com/article/archive/baghdad-burns-calgary-booms/.

Koram, K. (2020) 'Britain Needs a Truth and Reconciliation Commission, Not Another Racism Inquiry', *The Guardian*, 16 June. www.theguardian.com/commentisfree/2020/jun/16/britain-truth-reconciliation-commission-racism-imperial.

Krenak, A. (2020) *Ideas to Postpone the End of the World*. Translated by A. Doyle. Toronto: Anansi International.

Krug, D. (2006) 'Ecological Restoration: Mierle Ukeles, Flow City'. www.greenmuseum.org/c/aen/Issues/ukeles.php.

Lavery, C. (ed.) (2018) *Performance and Ecology: What Can Theatre Do?* Abingdon: Routledge.

L'Heureux, M. A. (2012) 'Infrastructure, Social Injustice, and the City: Parsing the Wisdom of Jane Jacobs', in S. Hirt and D. Zahm (eds) *The Urban Wisdom of Jane Jacobs*. New York: Routledge, pp. 101–121.

Massey, D. B. (1999) 'On Space and the City', in D. B. Massey, J. Allen and S. Pile (eds) *City Worlds*. London: Routledge, pp. 153–171.

Massey, D. B. (2011) *World City*. Cambridge: Polity.

May, T. J. (2020) *Earth Matters on Stage: Ecology and Environment in American Theater*. Abingdon: Routledge.

McCormack, P. A. (2017) 'Walking the Land: Aboriginal Trails, Cultural Landscapes, and Archaeological Studies for Impact Assessment', *Archaeologies*, 13(1), pp. 110–135. https://doi.org/10.1007/s11759-017-9309-7.

McKittrick, K. (2013) 'Plantation Futures', *Small Axe: A Caribbean Journal of Criticism*, 17(3), pp. 1–15. https://doi.org/10.1215/07990537-2378892.

Nesta (2023) 'The Strategy Room'. www.nesta.org.uk/project/strategyroom/.

Nixon, R. (2013) *Slow Violence and the Environmentalism of the Poor*. Cambridge, MA: Harvard University Press.

Nolan, Y. (2013) *The Unplugging*. Toronto: Playwrights Canada Press.

Nolan, Y. (2015) *Medicine Shows: Indigenous Performance Culture*. Toronto: Playwrights Canada Press.

Okwuosa, T. (2013) 'Environmental Challenges as Creative Muse: The Installation and Performance Art of Bright Ugochukwu Eke', *Academic Journal of Interdisciplinary Studies*, 2(3), pp. 63–70.

Onwueme, O. T. (2002) *Then She Said It*. San Francisco: African Heritage Press.

Osuoka, I. (2024) 'Shell's Exit Scam', *Africa Is a Country*, 12 December. https://africasacountry.com/2024/12/shells-exit-scam.

Platform (2005) 'Nigeria Ten Years On', *Carbon Web Newsletter, Issue 2*. https://platformlondon.org/nigeria-ten-years-on/?hilite=carbon+web+newsletter.

Platform (2024) 'The Carbon Web'. https://platformlondon.org/about-us/platform-the-carbon-web/.

Pretelin-Estéves, A. (2023) 'Proyecto Tejidos: Sullivan Garden of Art – Ecoscenographic Actions to Design Restorative Territories', *Prague Quadrennial 2023 Programme*. https://pq.cz/prague-quadrennial-2023/projects-2023/performance-space-exhibition/proyecto-tejidos-sullivan-garden-of-art-ecoscenographic-actions-to-design-restorative-territories/.

Robinson, D. (2019) 'Speaking to Water, Singing to Stone: Peter Morin, Rebecca Belmore, and the Ontologies of Indigenous Modernity', in V. L. Levine and D. Robinson (eds) *Music and Modernity among First Peoples of North America*. Middletown, CT: Wesleyan University Press, pp. 220–239.

Rowell, A., Marriott, J. and Stockman, L. (2005) *The Next Gulf: London, Washington and Oil Conflict in Nigeria*. London: Constable.

Ryan, C. B. (2023) *Eco-performance, Art, and Spatial Justice in the US*. London: Routledge.

Scott-Bottoms, S. (2013) 'Art and Oil in a Cool Climate (Pt. 3)', *Performance Footprint*, 8 November. www.performancefootprint.co.uk/2013/11/art-and-oil-in-a-cool-climate-pt-3/.

Sherk, B. (2012) 'Crossroad Community: The Farm, 1977', in J. Kastner (ed.) *Nature*. London: Whitechapel Art Gallery, pp. 165–166.

Smith, N. (2008) *Uneven Development: Nature, Capital, and the Production of Space*. 3rd ed. Athens: University of Georgia Press.

Solnit, R. (2006) 'Three Who Made a Revolution', *The Nation*, 16 March. www.thenation.com/article/three-who-made-revolution/.

Spaid, S. (2012) *Green Acres: Artists Farming Fields, Greenhouses and Abandoned Lots*. Cincinnati, OH: Contemporary Arts Center.

Spalink, A. (2024) *Choreographing Dirt: Movement, Performance, and Ecology in the Anthropocene*. Abingdon: Routledge.

Standing, S. A. (2012) 'Earth First!'s "Crack the Dam" and the Aesthetics of Ecoactivist Performance', in W. Arons and T. J. May (eds) *Readings in Performance and Ecology*. New York: Palgrave Macmillan, pp. 147–158.

Sugimoto, T. (2023) 'Claiming Space, Land and Ecology: Mapping Geographies of Indigenous and Decolonial Urbanisms in Taipei', *International Journal of Urban and Regional Research*, 47(1), pp. 130–145. https://doi.org/10.1111/1468-2427.13131.

Swyngedouw, E. (2007) 'Impossible "Sustainability" and the Postpolitical Condition', in R. Krueger and D. Gibbs (eds) *The Sustainable Development Paradox: Urban Political Economy in the United States and Europe*. New York: the Guilford press, pp. 13–40.

Sze, J. (2007) *Noxious New York: The Racial Politics of Urban Health and Environmental Justice*. Cambridge; London: MIT Press.

Szeman, I. and Boyer, D. (eds) (2017) *Energy Humanities: An Anthology*. Baltimore, MD: Johns Hopkins University Press.

Thomas, A. (2016) 'Ecodramaturgy', in G. Cody and M. Cheng (eds) *Reading Contemporary Performance: Theatricality Across Genres*. London: Routledge, pp. 200–201.

Thrush, C.-P. (2016) *Indigenous London: Native Travellers at the Heart of Empire*. New Haven, CT: Yale University Press.

Todd, Z. (2016) 'Relationships', *Theorizing the Contemporary, Fieldsights*, January 21. https://culanth.org/fieldsights/relationships.

Tsing, A., Swanson, H., Gan, E., and Bubandt, N. (eds) (2017) *Arts of Living on a Damaged Planet*. Minneapolis: University of Minnesota press.

Ukeles, M. L. (1996) 'Flow City', *Grand Street*, (57), pp. 199–213. https://doi.org/10.2307/25008073.

Ukeles, M. L. (2012) 'Flow City (1983–91)', in J. Kastner (ed.) *Nature*. London: Whitechapel Art Gallery, pp. 42–43.

United Nations Statistics Division (2023) 'Goal 11: Sustainable Cities and Communities'. https://unstats.un.org/sdgs/report/2023/goal-11/#:~:text=The%20world's%20population%20reached%208,70%20per%20cent%20by%202050.

Watts, M. (2008) 'Sweet and Sour', in M. Watts and E. Kashi (eds) *Curse of the Black Gold: 50 Years of Oil in the Niger Delta*. Brooklyn, NY: PowerHouse Books, pp. 36–47.

Weintraub, L. (2012) *To Life!: Eco Art in Pursuit of a Sustainable Planet*. Berkeley: University of California Press.

Whybrow, N. (2011) *Art and the City*. London: Palgrave Macmillan.

Whyte, K. P. (2018) 'Indigenous Science (Fiction) for the Anthropocene: Ancestral Dystopias and Fantasies of Climate Change Crises', *Environment and Planning E: Nature and Space*, 1(1–2), pp. 224–242. https://doi.org/10.1177/2514848618777621.

Wildcat, D. R. (2009) *Red Alert! Saving the Planet with Indigenous Knowledge*. Golden, CO: Fulcrum.

Woynarski, L. (2020a) *Ecodramaturgies: Theatre, Performance and Climate Change*. London: Palgrave Macmillan.

Woynarski, L. (2020b) 'Towards Radical Coexistence in the City: Performing the Bio-urban in Bonnie Ora Sherk's *The Farm* and Mierle Laderman Ukeles's *Flow City*', *Performance Research*, 25(2), pp. 126–133. https://doi.org/10.1080/13528165.2020.1752585.

Woynarski, L. (2025) 'Decolonizing Ecodramaturgies in Sheila Ghelani's and Sue Palmer's Atmospheric Forces and Ray Young's Thirst Trap', in M. Fragkou and R. Benzie (eds) *The Methuen Drama Handbook of Women in Contemporary British Theatre*. London: Bloomsbury, pp. 217–230.

Yusoff, K. (2018) *A Billion Black Anthropocenes or None*. Minneapolis: University of Minnesota Press.

Acknowledgements

This work was written on Anishinabewaki, Haudenosaunee and Mississauga traditional lands.

Deepest gratitude to Trish Reid for her editorial support and Adelina Ong for her encouragement and accountability. Thanks to the University of Reading, Department of Film, Theatre & Television, my performance and ecology colleagues and especially all the artists included here. Much appreciation goes to my family: Kay, Jan, Ron and Caitlin.

Cambridge Elements

Theatre, Performance and the Political

Trish Reid
University of Reading

Trish Reid is Professor of Theatre and Performance and Head of the School of Arts and Communication Design at the University of Reading. She is the author of *The Theatre of Anthony Neilson* (2017), *Theatre & Scotland* (2013), *Theatre and Performance in Contemporary Scotland* (2024) and co-editor of the *Routledge Companion to Twentieth-Century British Theatre* (2024).

Liz Tomlin
University of Glasgow

Liz Tomlin is Professor of Theatre and Performance at the University of Glasgow. Monographs include *Acts and Apparitions: Discourses on the Real in Performance Practice and Theory* (2013) and *Political Dramaturgies and Theatre Spectatorship: Provocations for Change* (2019). She edited *British Theatre Companies 1995–2014* (2015) and was the writer and co-director with Point Blank Theatre from 1999–2009.

Advisory Board

Aylwyn Walsh, *University of Leeds*
Alyson Campbell, *University of Melbourne*
Ameet Parameswaran, *Jawaharlal Nehru University*
Awo Mana Asiedu, *University of Ghana*
Carol Martin, *New York University*
Caroline Wake, *University of New South Wales*
Chris Megson, *Royal Holloway, University of London*
Collette Conroy, *University of Cumbria*
Freddie Rokem, *Israel Institute for Advanced Studies, The Hebrew University of Jerusalem*
Jean Graham-Jones, *City University of New York*
Mireia Aragay, *University of Barcelona*
Patrick Lonergan, *University of Glasgow*
Rebekah Maggor, *Cornell University*
Severine Ruset, *University of Grenoble*
Ute Berns, *University of Hamburg*
Vicky Angelaki, *Mid Sweden University*
Yasushi Nagata, *University of Osaka*

About the Series

Elements in Theatre, Performance and the Political showcases ground-breaking research that responds urgently and critically to the defining political concerns, and approaches, of our time. International in scope, the series engages with diverse performance histories and intellectual traditions, contesting established histories and providing new critical perspectives.

Cambridge Elements

Theatre, Performance and the Political

Elements in the Series

Theatre Revivals for the Anthropocene
Patrick Lonergan

Re-imagining Independence in Contemporary Greek Theatre and Performance
Philip Hager

Performing Nationalism in Russia
Yana Meerzon

Crisis Theatre and The Living Newspaper
Sarah Jane Mullan and Sarah Bartley

Utpal Dutt and Political Theatre in Postcolonial India
Mallarika Sinha Roy

Decolonising African Theatre
Samuel Ravengai

The Festival of India: Development and Diplomacy at the End of the Cold War
Rashna Darius Nicholson

Theatres of Autofiction
Lianna Mark

Performance and Postsocialism in Postmillennial China
Rossella Ferrari

Staging Class Conflict in the UK
Liz Tomlin

Empire, Extraction and Power in the Festivals of Britain of 1951 and 2022
Caoimhe Mader McGuinness

Performing Urban Ecologies
Lisa Woynarski

A full series listing is available at: www.cambridge.org/ETPP

Printed by Libri Plureos GmbH in Hamburg, Germany